HARCOURT HORIZONS

United States History

Activity Book

Orlando Austin Chicago New York Toronto London San Diego

Visit *The Learning Site!*
www.harcourtschool.com

Printed in the United States of America

ISBN 0-15-322602-1

1 2 3 4 5 6 7 8 9 10 073 10 09 08 07 06 05 04 03 02

The activities in this book reinforce social studies concepts and skills in the **Harcourt Horizons: United States History**. There is one activity for each lesson and skill. In addition, chapter graphic organizers and test preparation pages are provided. Reproductions of the activity pages appear with answers in the Teacher's Edition.

Contents

·UNIT·

2

·UNIT·

3

·UNIT· 4

Chapter 8

Chapter 9

·UNIT· 5

Chapter 10

Chapter 11

·UNIT·

6

Chapter 12

Chapter 13

·UNIT·

7

Chapter 14

Chapter 15

·UNIT·

8

Chapter 16

Chapter 17

Chapter 18

Name ______________________________ Date ______________

Multiple-Choice Answer Sheet

Number your answers to match the question on the test page.

____ (A) (B) (C) (D)
____ (F) (G) (H) (J)
____ (A) (B) (C) (D)
____ (F) (G) (H) (J)
____ (A) (B) (C) (D)

____ (A) (B) (C) (D)
____ (F) (G) (H) (J)
____ (A) (B) (C) (D)
____ (F) (G) (H) (J)
____ (A) (B) (C) (D)

____ (A) (B) (C) (D)
____ (F) (G) (H) (J)
____ (A) (B) (C) (D)
____ (F) (G) (H) (J)
____ (A) (B) (C) (D)

____ (A) (B) (C) (D)
____ (F) (G) (H) (J)
____ (A) (B) (C) (D)
____ (F) (G) (H) (J)
____ (A) (B) (C) (D)

____ (A) (B) (C) (D)
____ (F) (G) (H) (J)
____ (A) (B) (C) (D)
____ (F) (G) (H) (J)
____ (A) (B) (C) (D)

____ (A) (B) (C) (D)
____ (F) (G) (H) (J)
____ (A) (B) (C) (D)
____ (F) (G) (H) (J)
____ (A) (B) (C) (D)

____ (A) (B) (C) (D)
____ (F) (G) (H) (J)
____ (A) (B) (C) (D)
____ (F) (G) (H) (J)
____ (A) (B) (C) (D)

____ (A) (B) (C) (D)
____ (F) (G) (H) (J)
____ (A) (B) (C) (D)
____ (F) (G) (H) (J)
____ (A) (B) (C) (D)

____ (A) (B) (C) (D)
____ (F) (G) (H) (J)
____ (A) (B) (C) (D)
____ (F) (G) (H) (J)
____ (A) (B) (C) (D)

____ (A) (B) (C) (D)
____ (F) (G) (H) (J)
____ (A) (B) (C) (D)
____ (F) (G) (H) (J)
____ (A) (B) (C) (D)

____ (A) (B) (C) (D)
____ (F) (G) (H) (J)
____ (A) (B) (C) (D)
____ (F) (G) (H) (J)
____ (A) (B) (C) (D)

____ (A) (B) (C) (D)
____ (F) (G) (H) (J)
____ (A) (B) (C) (D)
____ (F) (G) (H) (J)
____ (A) (B) (C) (D)

____ (A) (B) (C) (D)
____ (F) (G) (H) (J)
____ (A) (B) (C) (D)
____ (F) (G) (H) (J)
____ (A) (B) (C) (D)

____ (A) (B) (C) (D)
____ (F) (G) (H) (J)
____ (A) (B) (C) (D)
____ (F) (G) (H) (J)
____ (A) (B) (C) (D)

____ (A) (B) (C) (D)
____ (F) (G) (H) (J)
____ (A) (B) (C) (D)
____ (F) (G) (H) (J)
____ (A) (B) (C) (D)

____ (A) (B) (C) (D)
____ (F) (G) (H) (J)
____ (A) (B) (C) (D)
____ (F) (G) (H) (J)
____ (A) (B) (C) (D)

____ (A) (B) (C) (D)
____ (F) (G) (H) (J)
____ (A) (B) (C) (D)
____ (F) (G) (H) (J)
____ (A) (B) (C) (D)

____ (A) (B) (C) (D)
____ (F) (G) (H) (J)
____ (A) (B) (C) (D)
____ (F) (G) (H) (J)
____ (A) (B) (C) (D)

Name ______________________ Date ____________

Read a Map

Directions **Use the map to answer the questions that follow.**

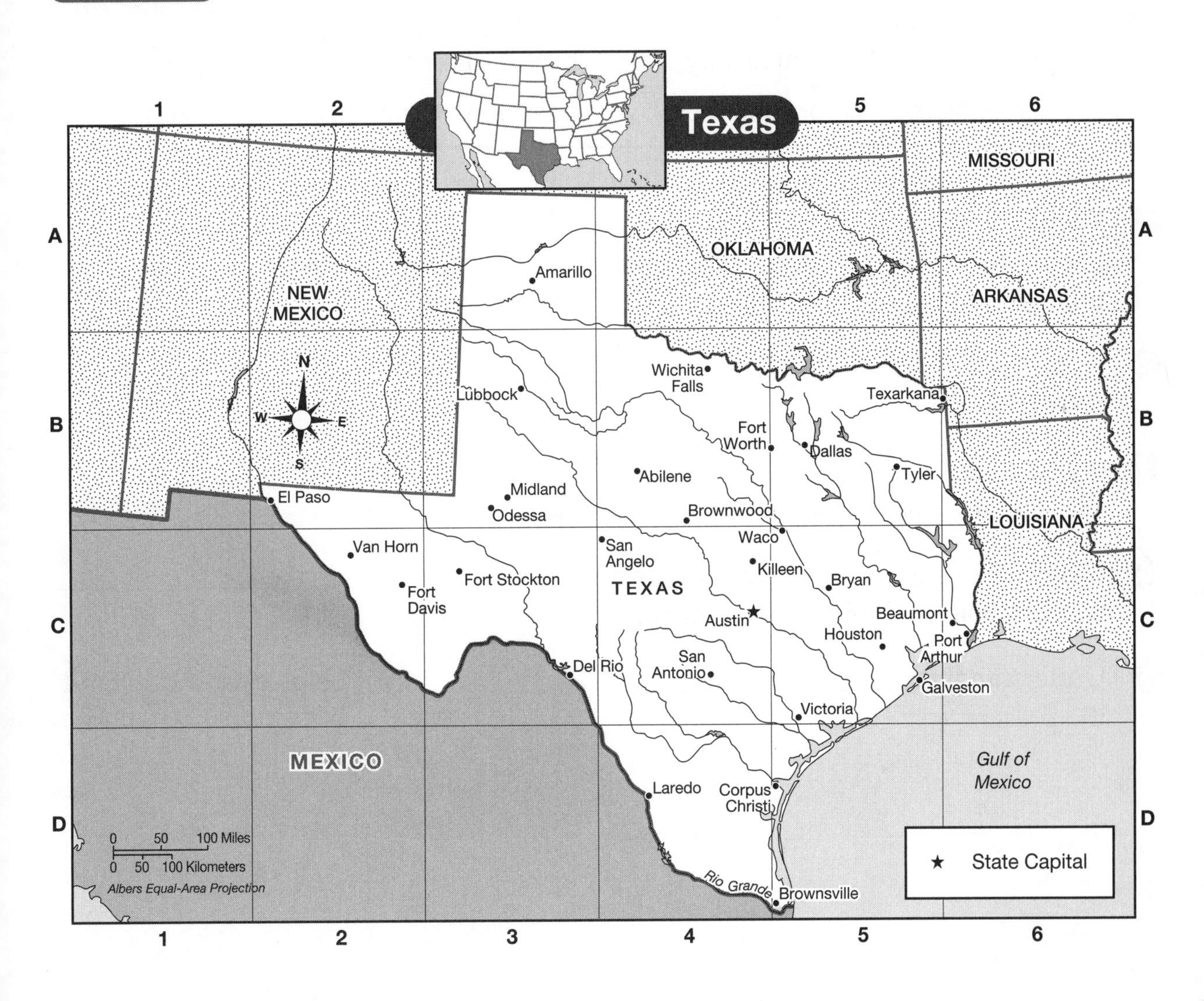

1. What is the capital of Texas? ______________________
2. What states border Texas? ______________________
3. What city is located at C5? ______________________
4. What body of water borders Texas? ______________________
5. About how many miles is it from Fort Davis to El Paso if you drive through Van Horn? ______________________

   What direction do you travel to get there? ______________________
6. What river forms the border between Texas and Mexico? ______________________

Name ____________________ Date __________

Why History Matters

Directions **Use the terms in the Word Bank to complete the sentences below.**

history	oral history	historical empathy	analyze
chronology	point of view	frames of reference	

1. People's ____________________ are based on where people were when an event happened and how they were involved with that event.

2. ____________________ is the order in which events happened.

3. A person's ____________________ is based on his or her age, gender, class, background, and experiences.

4. Historians listen to and read records of ____________________ to help them understand past events.

5. Understanding ____________________ helps you understand the present.

Name ____________________ Date ____________

Compare Primary and Secondary Sources

Directions **Use Captain Charles Sigsbee's letter and the *New York Times* article to answer the questions below.**

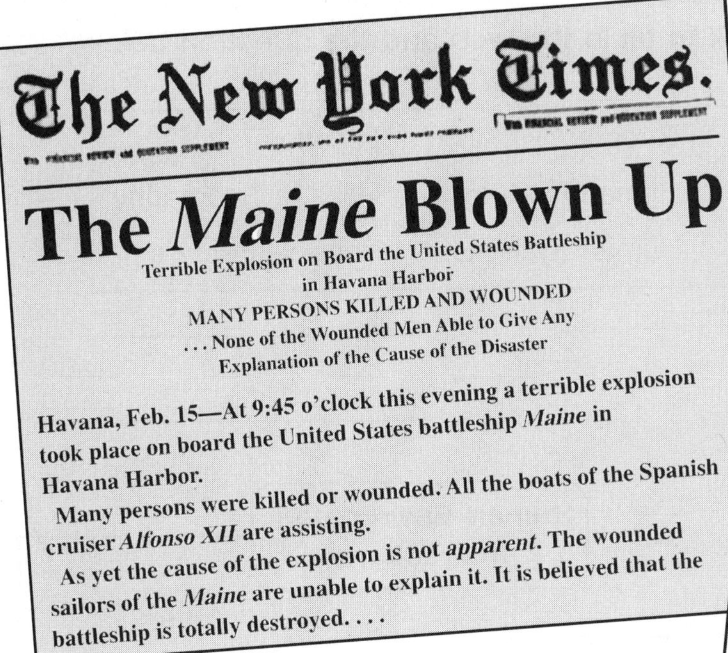

The New York Times.

The *Maine* Blown Up

Terrible Explosion on Board the United States Battleship in Havana Harbor

MANY PERSONS KILLED AND WOUNDED

. . . None of the Wounded Men Able to Give Any Explanation of the Cause of the Disaster

Havana, Feb. 15—At 9:45 o'clock this evening a terrible explosion took place on board the United States battleship *Maine* in Havana Harbor.

Many persons were killed or wounded. All the boats of the Spanish cruiser *Alfonso XII* are assisting.

As yet the cause of the explosion is not *apparent*. The wounded sailors of the *Maine* are unable to explain it. It is believed that the battleship is totally destroyed. . . .

"... I felt the crash of the explosion. It was a ... roar of immense volume, largely metallic in character. It was succeeded by a ... trembling and lurching motion of the vessel, then ... an eclipse of the electric lights and intense darkness within the cabin. I knew immediately that the MAINE had been blown up and that she was sinking ...."

Captain Charles D. Sigsbee,
MAINE Commanding Officer

1. What source lists where the explosion occurred? ____________________

2. How did Captain Sigsbee know the *Maine* was sinking?

____

3. What does Captain Sigsbee's letter tell you that the *New York Times* article does not? ____________________

4. How is the tone of the newspaper article different from the tone of the letter?

____

Name ______________________ Date ______________

Why Geography Matters

Geography is the study of the Earth's surface and the way people use it. Geographers use many different themes and topics to study a place. Understanding these themes and topics and their relationships will help you to better understand geography.

Directions **Use the Word Bank to fill in the web and the question below.**

Places and Regions	Geography	Location
Movement	Human Feature	Uses of Geography
Environment and Society	Human Systems	Physical Feature

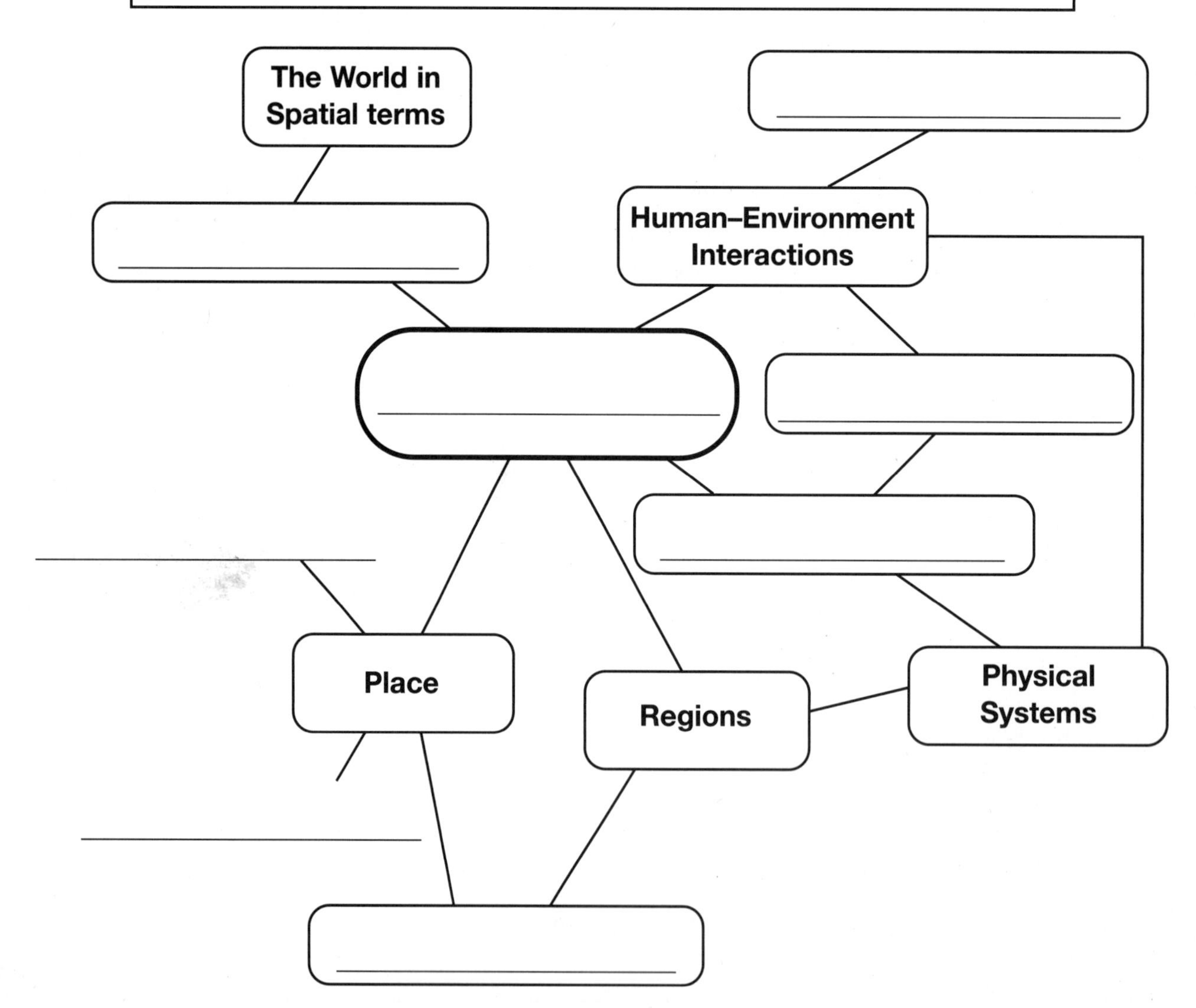

Knowing how to use maps, globes, and geographic tools helps you understand the

______________________ and prepares you for life.

Name ______________________ Date ____________

Why Economics, Civics, and Government Matter

Directions **Read the flow chart and answer the questions below.**

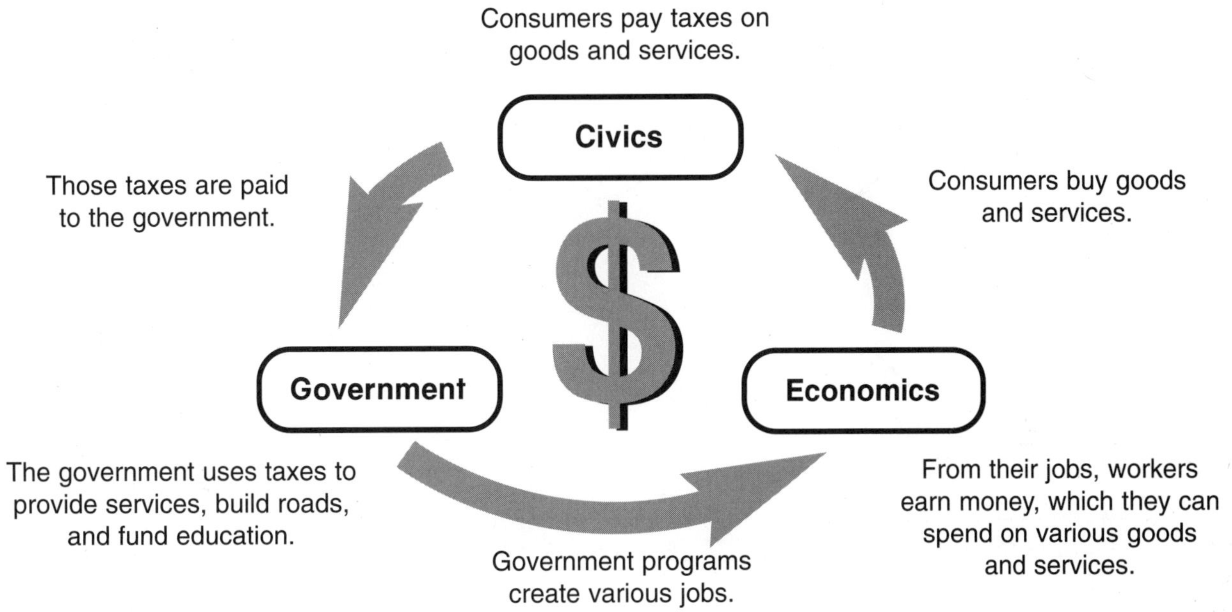

Consumers pay taxes on goods and services.

Civics

Consumers buy goods and services.

Economics

From their jobs, workers earn money, which they can spend on various goods and services.

Government programs create various jobs.

Government

The government uses taxes to provide services, build roads, and fund education.

Those taxes are paid to the government.

$

1. What happens when fewer jobs are available and unemployment goes up?

____

____

2. What step happens between when the government creates jobs and when consumers buy goods and services? ______________________________

____

3. What happens when the government raises taxes? ______________________________

____

____

4. What would happen if consumers did not pay taxes on goods and services?

____

____

Name ______________________ Date ______________

Land and Regions

Directions **Look at each numbered place on the map. Find the word in the box that describes the place. Then write the word on the line with the same number.**

sea level	basin	mountain range	plain
valley	volcano	piedmont	plateau

1 ______________________ 4 ______________________

2 ______________________ 5 ______________________

3 ______________________ 6 ______________________

Directions **Show the meaning of the words *piedmont* and *plateau* by using each word in a sentence.**

____

____

____

 Use after reading Chapter 1, Lesson 1, pages 18–23.

Name ______________________ Date ______________

MAP AND GLOBE SKILLS

Use Elevation Maps

Directions **Study the elevation map and answer the questions below.**

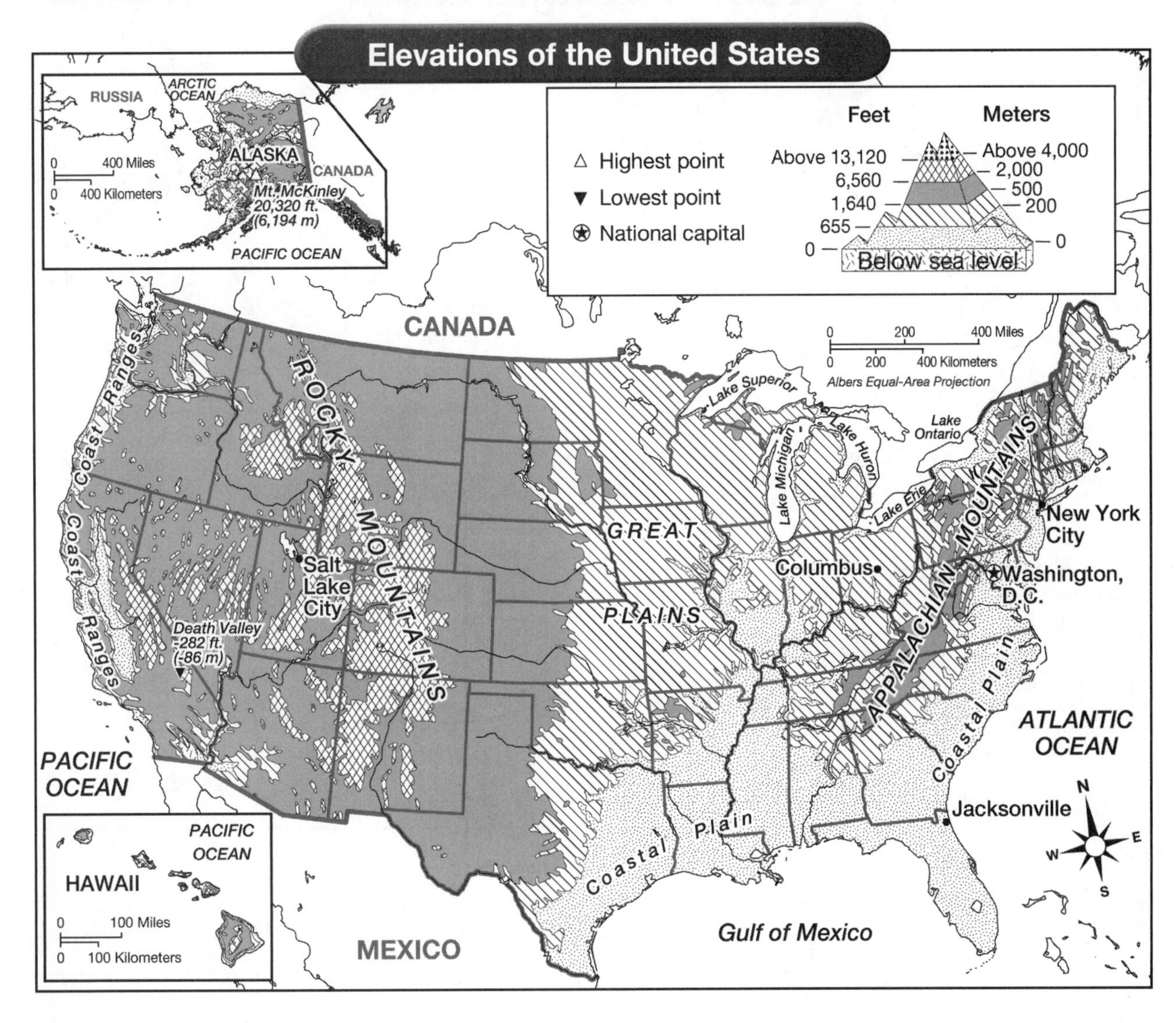

1. Which city has the higher elevation: Jacksonville, Florida, or Columbus, Ohio?

____

2. What is the elevation range of the Rocky Mountains? ______________________

____

3. In what state can you find an inland location that is lower than sea level? What is the name of the location? ______________________

Name ______________________________ Date ______________

Bodies of Water

Directions **Use the map to answer the questions below.**

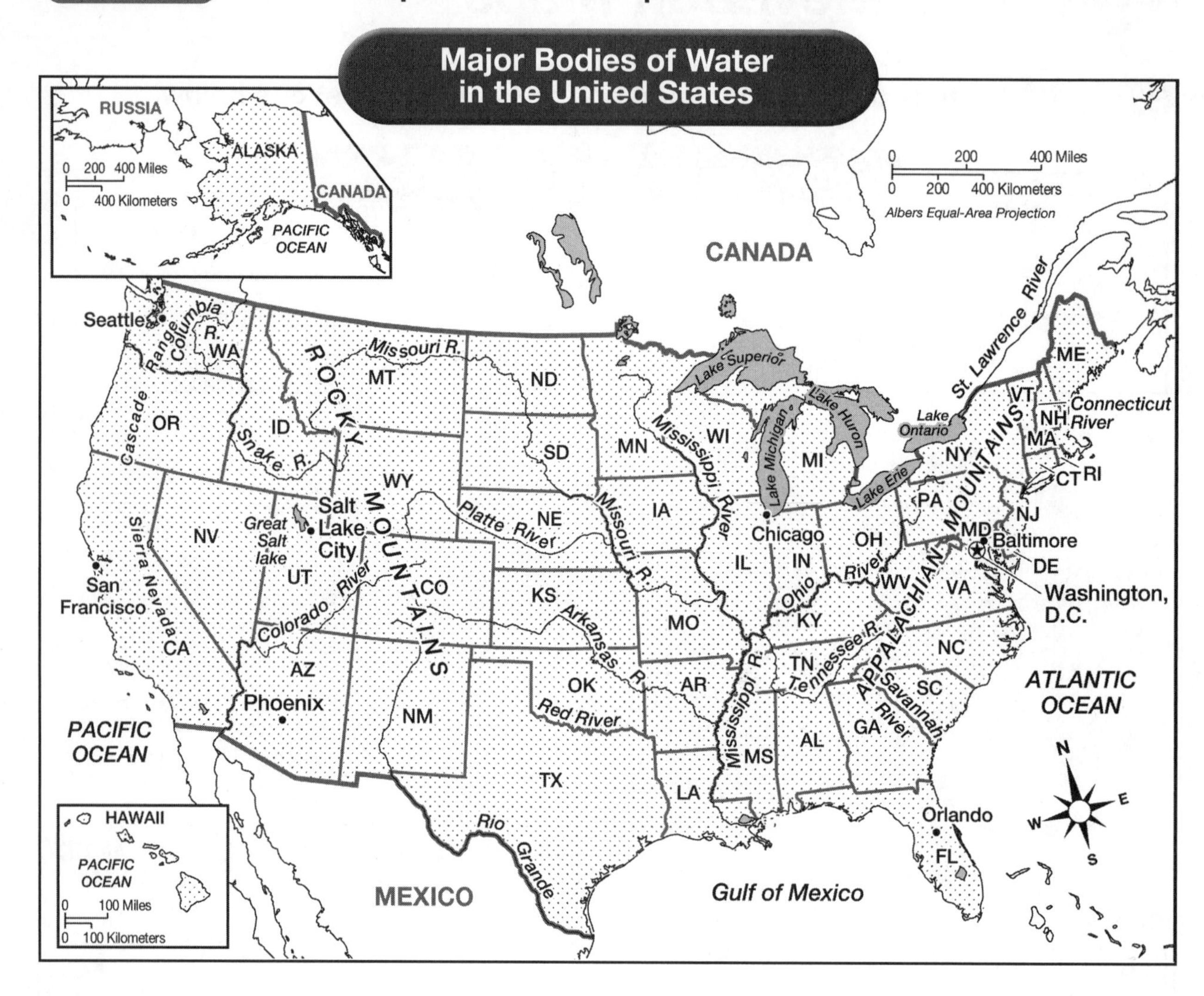

1. Name the Great Lakes. ______________________________

____

2. Name the states that border the Gulf of Mexico. ______________________________

____

3. Name three tributaries of the Mississippi River. ______________________________

____

4. What states does the Arkansas River flow through? ______________________________

____

Use after reading Chapter 1, Lesson 2, pages 26–32.

Name ______________________________ Date ______________

Climate and Vegetation Regions

Directions **Use the map to fill in the chart below.**

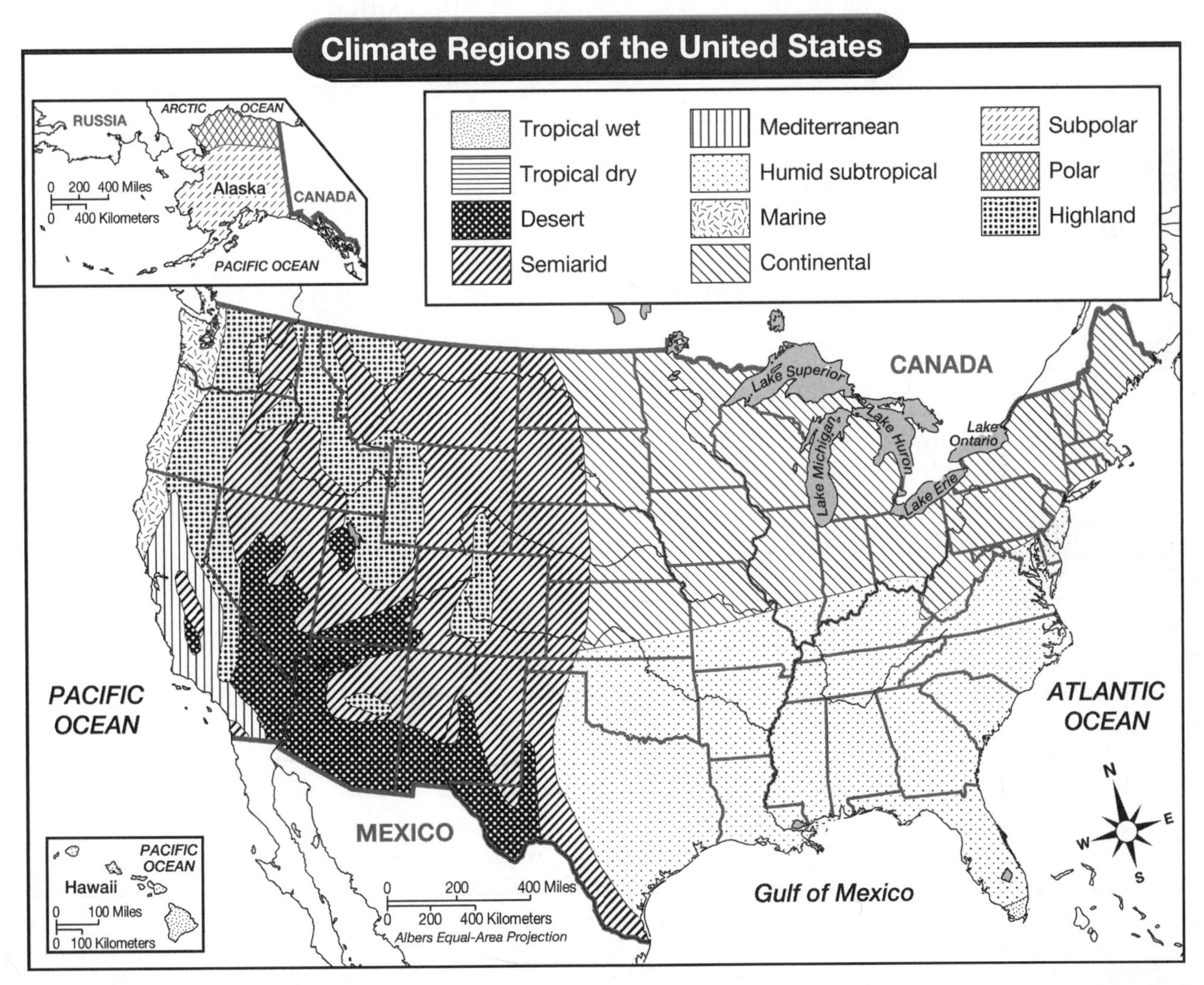

Place or Region	Climate Region
Southeastern United States	
Southwestern United States	
Pacific Coast	
Atlantic Coast	
Alaska	
Hawaii	

Name ______________________ Date ____________

Using the Land

Directions **Write the correct answer in the space provided.**

1. When people change their environment, they ______________________ it.

2. A resource that cannot be made again by nature or people is called a ______________________ resource.

3. A ______________________ resource is one that can be made again by nature or by people.

4. Farmers often modify the soil by adding ______________________ to grow better crops.

5. Some farmers modify their land with ______________________, which brings water to dry areas.

Directions **Write the name of the resource in the correct column.**

air	iron	trees	zinc	fish
sunlight	oil	natural gas	plants	limestone
water	gold	copper	coal	wind

Renewable Resources	Nonrenewable Resources

Use after reading Chapter 1, Lesson 4, pages 40–43.

Name ______________________ Date ______________

Where People Live and Work

Directions **Read each clue. Then use the clues to complete the word puzzle below.**

relative location	crossroads	suburban	rural
metropolitan	railroad	farm	economic

ACROSS

3. The location of a place compared to one or more other places
5. A place where crops are raised
6. Kind of area made up of a city and its suburbs
7. A place where two roads or railroads intersect

DOWN

1. Kind of area surrounding a large city
2. A system that moves goods overland
3. Kind of area located in the country, away from cities
4. Region named for the work done or product made within it

Name ______________________ Date ______________

MAP AND GLOBE SKILLS

Use Latitude and Longitude

Directions **Location is important to people choosing a place to live. People may choose to live and work near a coast or near a major transportation route. Use the map to fill in the chart below.**

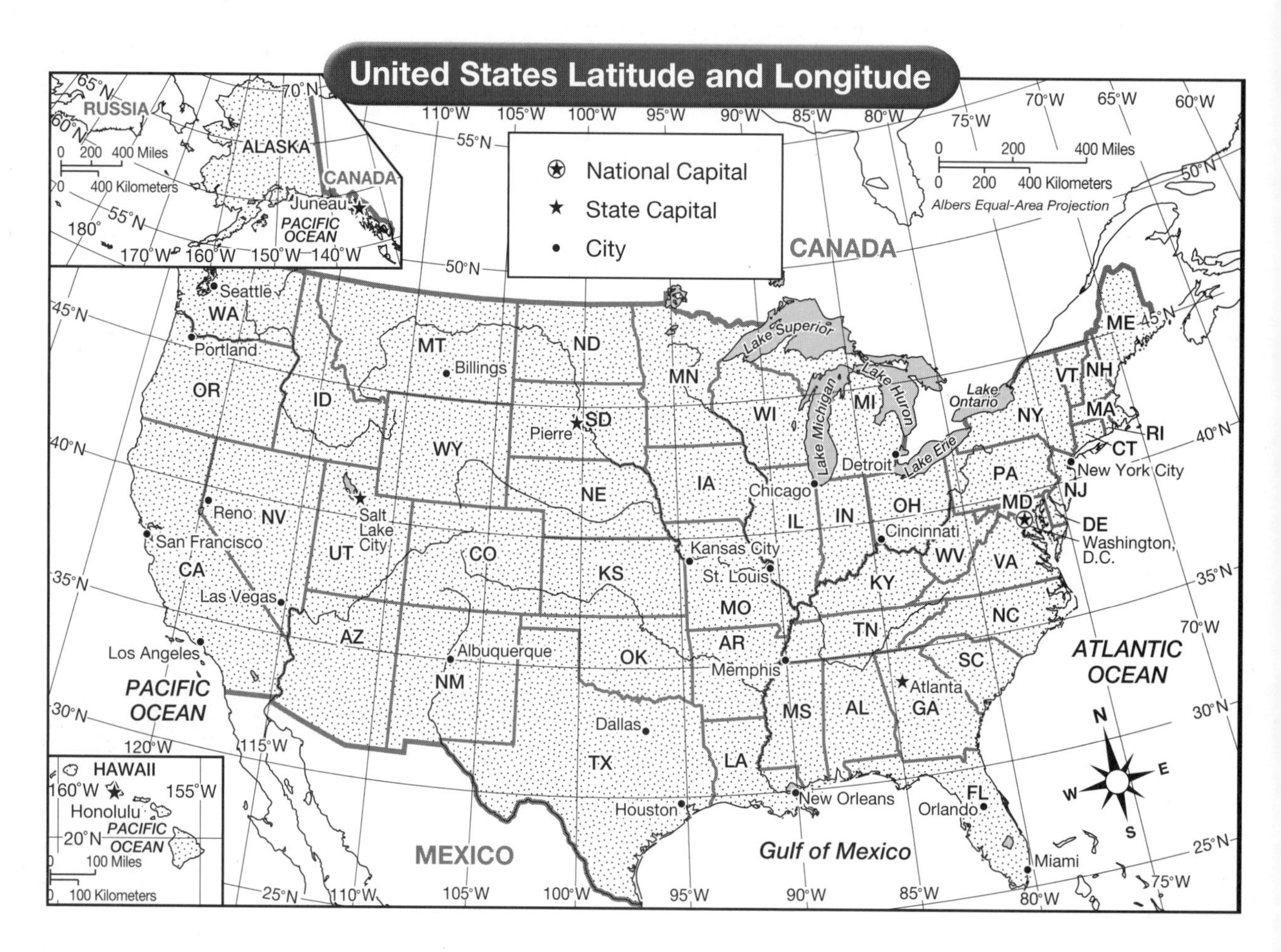

City	Latitude	Longitude
New York City, NY		
Los Angeles, CA		
Chicago, IL		
New Orleans, LA		

Use after reading Chapter 1, Skill Lesson, pages 50–51.

Name ____________________ Date ____________

Regions of the United States

Directions **Complete this graphic organizer to show that you have identified the main idea and supporting details in this chapter.**

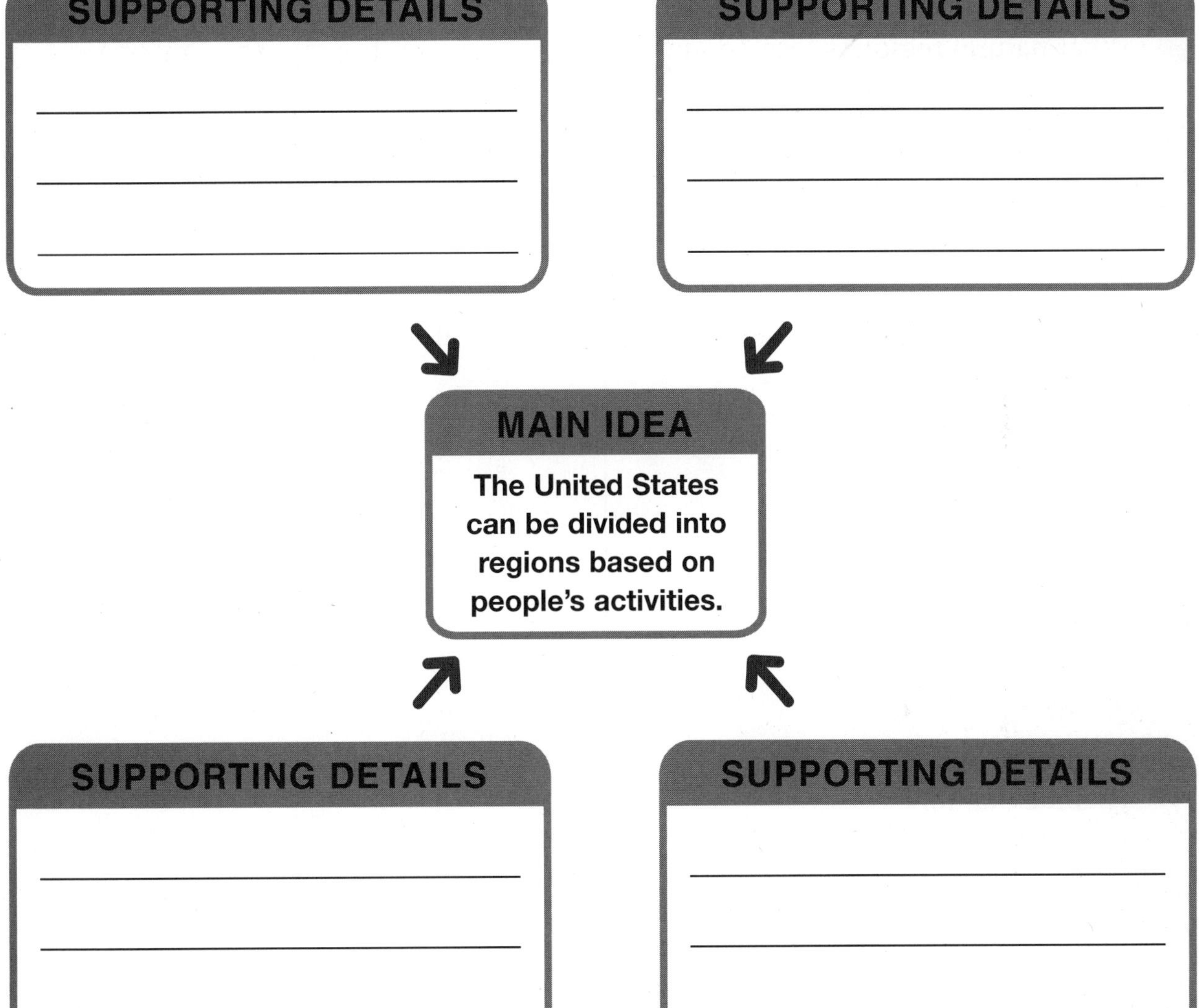

Use after reading Chapter 1, pages 17–51.

Name ______________________ Date __________

Test Preparation

Directions **Read each question and choose the best answer. Then fill in the circle for the answer you have chosen. Be sure to fill in the circle completely.**

1. What natural region is located at or near the foot of a mountain?
   - Ⓐ peak
   - Ⓑ hill
   - Ⓒ piedmont
   - Ⓓ humidity

2. Which of these is **not** the name of a landform?
   - Ⓕ plain
   - Ⓖ climate
   - Ⓗ mountain
   - Ⓙ valley

3. Which of these cause ocean currents?
   - Ⓐ location
   - Ⓑ elevation
   - Ⓒ precipitation
   - Ⓓ wind

4. Places in the rain shadow of a mountain receive very little—
   - Ⓕ sunlight.
   - Ⓖ precipitation.
   - Ⓗ wind.
   - Ⓙ temperature.

5. Another name for *grassland* is—
   - Ⓐ prairie.
   - Ⓑ mesquite.
   - Ⓒ lichens.
   - Ⓓ tundra.

Use after reading Chapter 1, pages 16–53.

Name ______________________________ Date ______________

The First to Arrive

Directions Read the list of statements below about the arrival of ancient peoples in the Americas. In the spaces provided, write *LB* if a statement refers to the land bridge theory, *EA* if it refers to the early-arrival theory, or *O* if it refers to origin theory.

1. ______ The Blackfoot people tell a story of Old Man the Creator.
2. ______ Some scientists believe that between 12,000 and 40,000 years ago, Asian hunting groups reached present-day Alaska.
3. ______ Recent discoveries support the idea that ancient peoples came by boat to the Americas.
4. ______ Archaeologists in Brazil have discovered artifacts that may be 30,000 years old.
5. ______ According to the Hurons, land was formed from soil found in a turtle's claws.
6. ______ There are many people today who believe that the first Americans did not come from Asia or anywhere else.
7. ______ Following a path between glaciers, hunters slowly made their way farther into the Americas.
8. ______ At Meadowcroft Rock Shelter archaeologists discovered a few artifacts that are more than 19,000 years old.
9. ______ Many present-day Native Americans believe that their people have always lived in the Americas.
10. ______ After thousands of years, Asian hunters reached what is today Alaska.
11. ______ In Monte Verde, Chile, archaeologists uncovered artifacts, animal bones, and a child's foot print that had been there for at least 13,000 years.
12. ______ At several different times the level of the oceans dropped causing dry land to appear between Asia and North America.

Name ______________________________ Date ______________

CHART AND GRAPH SKILLS

Read Time Lines

Directions **The time line on this page lists events that happened in the Americas. Study the time line and then answer the questions below.**

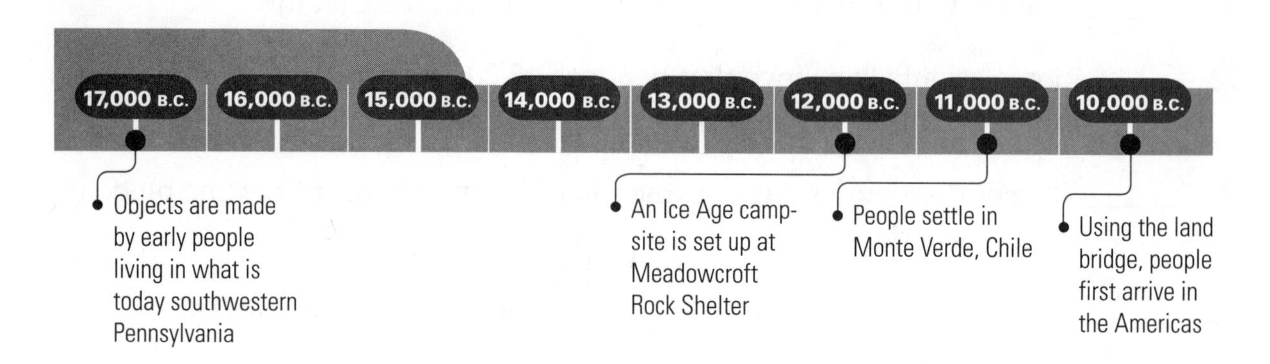

1. Artifacts found in Monte Verde, Chile, provide proof that people were there as long ago as ______________________________.

2. Artifacts found at the Meadowcroft Rock Shelter suggest that people were living there in ______________________________.

3. The oldest objects found at Meadowcroft Rock Shelter date back to ______________________________.

4. The land-bridge theory says people first arrived in the Americas around ______________________________.

Use after reading Chapter 2, Skill Lesson, pages 60–61.

Name ______________________________ Date ______________

Ancient Indians

Directions **Use the Word Bank below to complete a paragraph about the different cultures of the Olmecs, Maya, Mound Builders, and Anasazi.**

technology	nomads	Mound Builders	agriculture	civilization	extinct
Anasazi	classes	slaves	pueblos	tribes	

The Olmec ______________________ lived in what is now southeastern Mexico. Because the Olmecs remained in one place, they were not considered ______________________ . The Olmecs shared their ideas with other cultures, or ______________________ , such as the Maya. The Olmecs and Maya were divided into separate social ______________________ , based upon people's occupations. At the bottom of Mayan society were ______________________ , or people forced to work against their will. At about the same time, a group of Native Americans began building a society in what is today the southeastern United States. These people were known as ______________________ because of the earthen mounds they built as places of burial or worship. Hundreds of years later, a group called the ______________________ built a society in what is today the southwestern United States. In this society, people lived in groups of houses built closely together. These houses were called ______________________ , the Spanish word for "village."

Name ______________________________ Date ______________

MAP AND GLOBE SKILLS

Use a Cultural Map

Directions **Use the map to answer the following questions.**

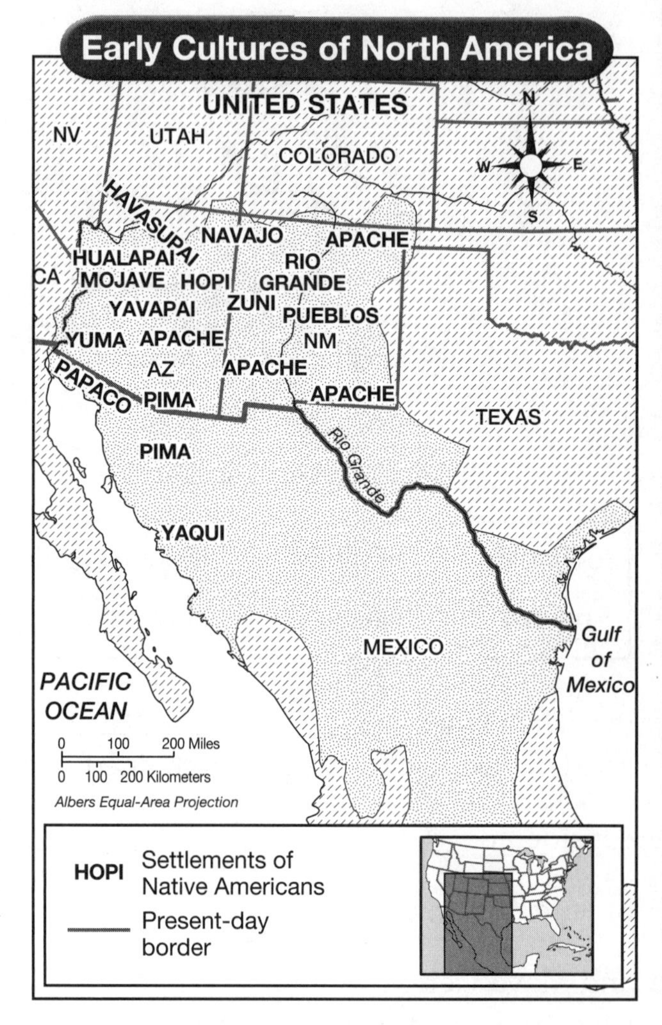

1. According to the map, Native Americans of the Desert Southwest lived in parts of which present-day states? ______________________________

____

2. What generalization can you make about the location of settlements in the Desert Southwest?

____

____

____

____

____

3. Why do you think the Navajos learned certain customs from the Hopis rather than from the Pima?

____

____

4. What generalization can you make about the ways of life of Native Americans who lived in the Southwest? ______________________________

____

____

Use after reading Chapter 2, Skill Lesson, pages 68–69.

Name ________________________________ Date ______________

The Desert Southwest

Directions **On the blanks provided, write the word or name that best completes each sentence. Some letters in your answers will have numbers underneath them. Write these letters on the numbered blanks below, and you will find the name of a region in the United States.**

1. Many Native Americans who lived in the d__ __ __(1) __ __ t were able to change the way they lived and adjust to the land and its resources.

2. Native American tribes such as the Hopis and Zunis lived in __ __ __ b __ o(2) __ .

3. They learned that by growing a __ __(3) __ p l __ __ of food they could survive during times of harsh weather.

4. Many of the crops grown by Native Americans were s __(4) __ __ __ e foods such as corn, beans, and squash.

5. The Hopis worshiped many gods and spirits, including __ __ __ h(5) __ __ a __ , who were believed to visit their world once a year.

6. Around the year 1025, the Hopis were joined on their lands by __ __ __(6) c __ m __ __ __ , such as the Navajos.

7. The Navajos settled in an area known as the F __ __ __ __ __ __ __ __(7) __ __ region, where parts of present-day Arizona, Colorado, New Mexico, and Utah meet.

8. The Navajos learned many customs from the Hopis, including how to build dome-shaped shelters called __ __ __ __ n __(8).

9. The Navajos' use of Hopi ways was an example of their ability to __ __ __ __ __(9) to desert life.

__	__	__	__	__	__	__	__	__
1	2	3	4	5	6	7	8	9

Name ______________________ Date ____________

The Northwest Coast and the Arctic

Directions **Complete the following chart by comparing and contrasting the ways of life of the Northwest Coast and Arctic Indians, and then answer the questions that follow.**

Northwest Coast Indians	Arctic Indians
lived in a land of rivers and forests	
	lived in igloos, tents, and huts
had many resources	
hunted salmon, other fish, and whales	
	used animal parts to build shelters and make tools

1. Contrast the living environments of the Northwest Coast and Arctic Indians.

____

____

2. Describe the resources that the Northwest Coast and Arctic Indians used for building shelters and making tools. ______________________

____

____

3. Using the information from the chart as a guide, write a paragraph comparing and contrasting the ways of life of the Northwest Coast and Arctic Indians.

____

____

____

____

____

____

Use after reading Chapter 2, Lesson 4, pages 76–80.

Name ______________________________ Date ______________

The Plains

Directions **Match the items below to the buffalo parts from which they were made. You will use some parts more than once. Then answer the questions.**

A. hides

B. stomach

C. hair

D. bones and horns

E. meat

_____ clothing

_____ bags for water

_____ cord

_____ needles and tools

_____ blankets

_____ fresh or dried food

_____ moccasins

_____ tepee coverings

1. Of the parts listed above, which was used for the most purposes?

____

2. What parts would the Plains Indians have used to make their shelters?

____

3. What buffalo part do you think was most useful? ______________

____

____

Name ______________________ Date ____________

The Eastern Woodlands

Directions **Read the paragraph. Then answer the questions that follow.**

In the late 1500s, Iroquois villages often battled among themselves. Often, these battles grew out of small disputes that led to ill will between villages. According to tradition, a Huron named Deganawida believed that the battles must stop if the Iroquois tribes were to protect their ways of life from European newcomers. Deganawida persuaded a Mohawk leader named Hiawatha to join him in spreading the message throughout Iroquois country that "All shall receive the Great Law and labor together for the welfare of man."

The result of their effort was a confederation called the Iroquois League, made up of the Five Nations of the Seneca, the Cayuga, the Onondaga, the Oneida, and the Mohawk. A few years later a sixth nation, the Tuscarora, joined the confederacy.

Each nation in the league governed itself, and matters often were settled by unanimous vote. Very important matters, such as war, were left for discussion by a Great Council of 50 chiefs.

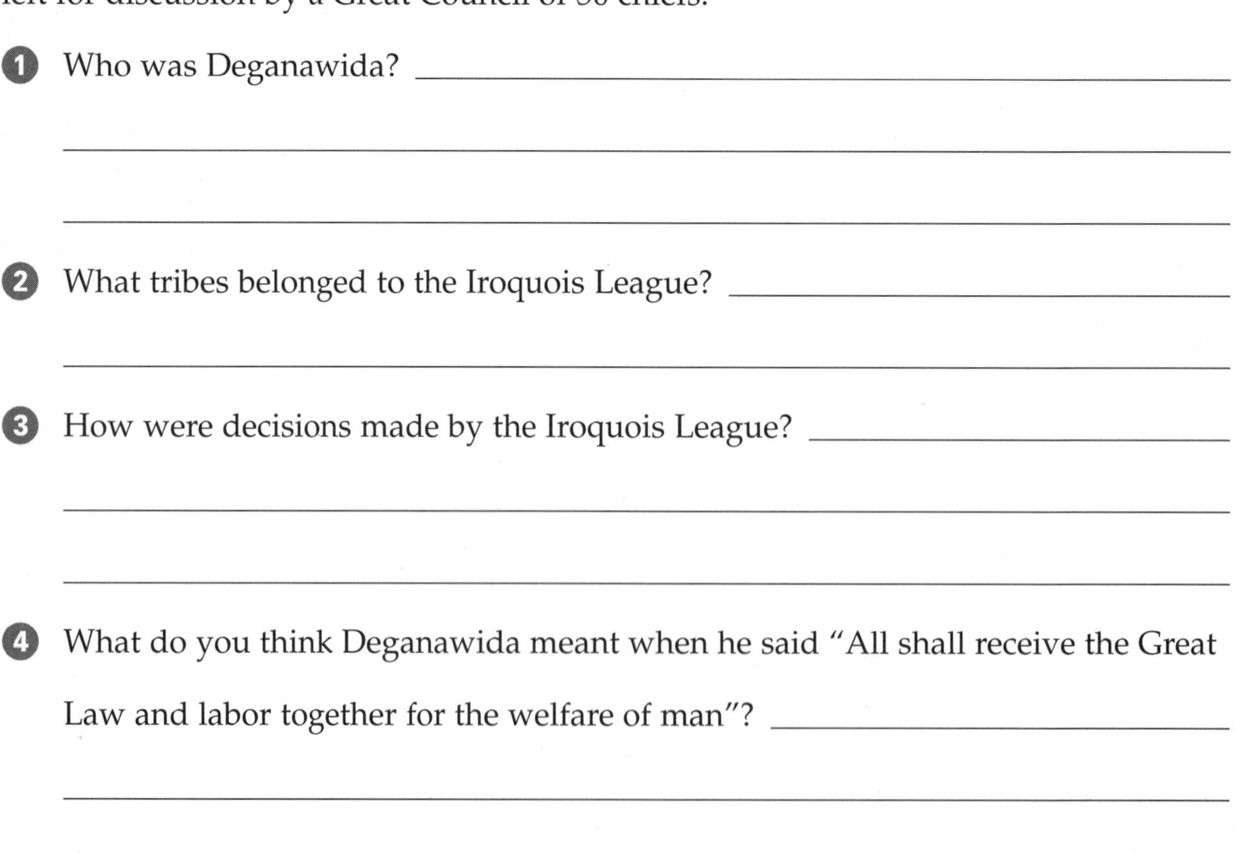

1. Who was Deganawida? ______________________

____

____

2. What tribes belonged to the Iroquois League? ______________________

____

3. How were decisions made by the Iroquois League? ______________________

____

____

4. What do you think Deganawida meant when he said "All shall receive the Great Law and labor together for the welfare of man"? ______________________

____

____

Use after reading Chapter 2, Lesson 6, pages 86–90.

Name ______________________ Date ______________

CITIZENSHIP SKILLS
Resolve Conflict

Directions **Complete the graphic organizer below. For each step, write the decisions that led to the formation of the Iroquois League.**

ALL SIDES CLEARLY STATE WANTS AND NEEDS

____

____

↓

ALL SIDES DECIDE WHAT IS MOST IMPORTANT

____

____

↓

ALL SIDES PLAN AND DISCUSS POSSIBLE COMPROMISES

____

____

____

↓

ALL SIDES PLAN A LASTING COMPROMISE

____

____

Use after reading Chapter 2, Skill Lesson, page 91.

Name ______________________________ Date ______________

Indians of the Plains and Northwest Coast

Directions **Complete this graphic organizer to compare and contrast the Indians of the Plains and the Indians of the Northwest Coast.**

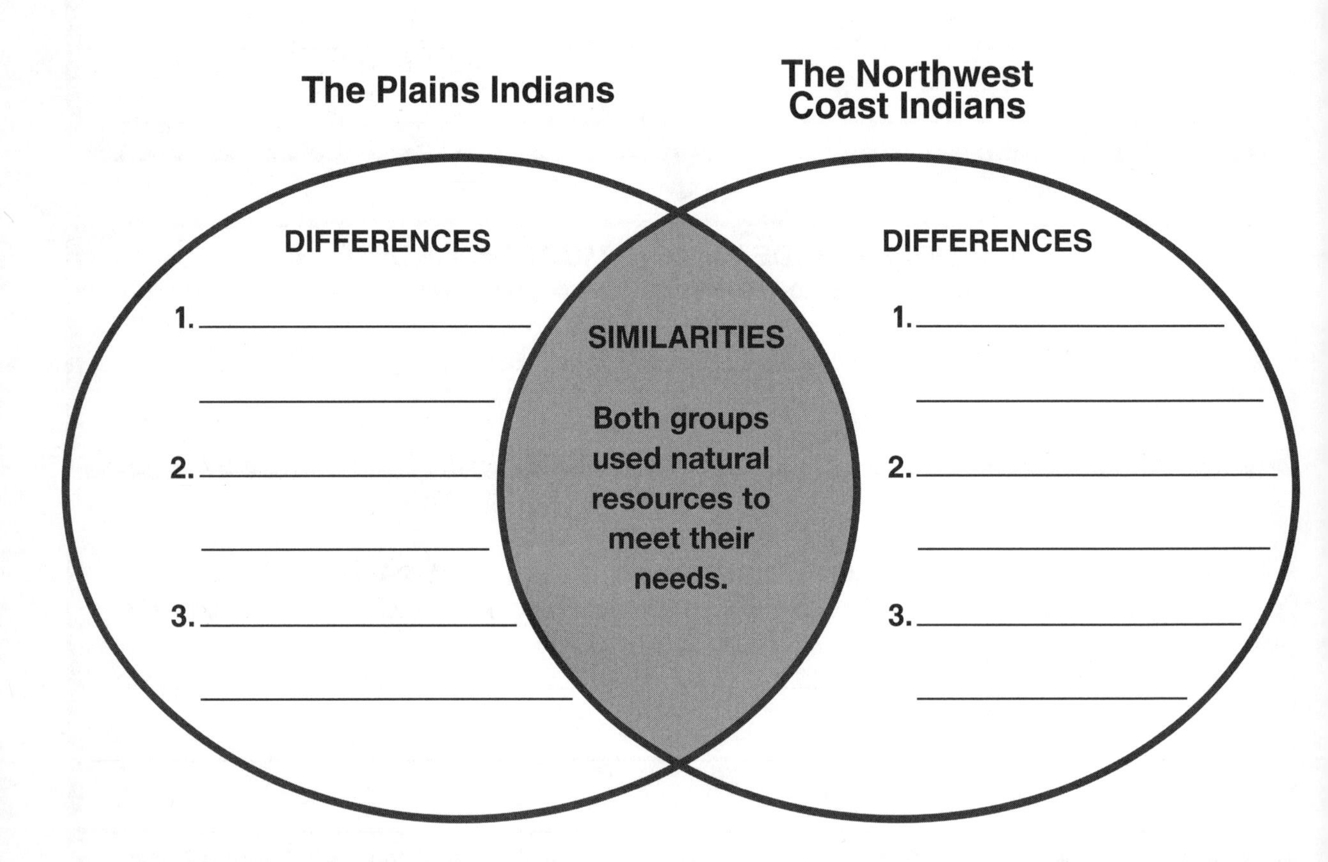

Use after reading Chapter 2, pages 55–91.

• CHAPTER • 2

Name ______________________ Date ____________

Test Preparation

Directions **Read each question and choose the best answer. Then fill in the circle for the answer you have chosen. Be sure to fill in the circle completely.**

1. Which of the following explains early settlement in the Americas?
   - Ⓐ land-bridge theory
   - Ⓑ early-arrival theory
   - Ⓒ origin stories
   - Ⓓ all of the above

2. Which of the following shows the correct order of the development of civilizations in the Americas?
   - Ⓕ the Olmecs, the Maya, the Mound Builders, the Anasazi
   - Ⓖ the Olmecs, the Mound Builders, the Maya, the Anasazi
   - Ⓗ the Maya, the Olmecs, the Mound Builders, the Anasazi
   - Ⓙ the Olmecs, the Maya, the Anasazi, the Mound Builders

3. Which statement **best** describes the people of the Desert Southwest?
   - Ⓐ They adapted their ways of life to fit their environment.
   - Ⓑ They believed in gods of the sun, rain, and Earth.
   - Ⓒ They lived in dome-shaped shelters called hogans.
   - Ⓓ They shared certain customs.

4. Unlike the Northwest Coast Indians, the Arctic Indians—
   - Ⓕ used animals for most of their food, shelter, and tools.
   - Ⓖ lived in villages.
   - Ⓗ hunted whales.
   - Ⓙ raised their food on farms.

5. The Iroquois League—
   - Ⓐ was a confederation made up of the Five Nations.
   - Ⓑ relied on a Great Council to make important decisions.
   - Ⓒ put an end to most Iroquois fighting.
   - Ⓓ all of the above.

Name ______________________________ Date ______________

The World in the 1400s

Directions **Use words and phrases from the Word Bank to complete the chart.**

Aztecs	Mali	Ghana	Renaissance	Lake Texcoco
Portugal	Timbuktu	quipus	Vijayanagar	Songhay Empire
Cuzco	Incas	Zheng He	carved ivory	Johannes Gutenberg
compass	China	Benin	the Bible	Andes Mountains
junks				

The Americas	Europe	Asia	Africa

Directions **Write your answer to each question.**

1. In what ways did the peoples of the Americas, Europe, Asia, and Africa interact with one another in the 1400s? ______________________________

____

____

2. How did China change after the death of its ruler Yong Le?

____

____

____

Use after reading Chapter 3, Lesson 1, pages 106–111.

Name ______________________ Date ______________

MAP AND GLOBE SKILLS

Follow Routes on a Map

The Chinese Emperor sent admiral Zheng He, an explorer, on several voyages to explore the oceans surrounding China. From 1405 to 1433, Zheng He's fleets sailed on at least seven voyages. The admiral and his crew used wooden sailing ships called junks. The junks had flat bottoms, high masts, and square sails. Zheng He's expeditions took him to trading centers along the coast of China, as well as to the cities of Majapahit, Calicut, Hormuz, Mecca, and Mogadishu.

Directions **Use the map to help you answer the questions.**

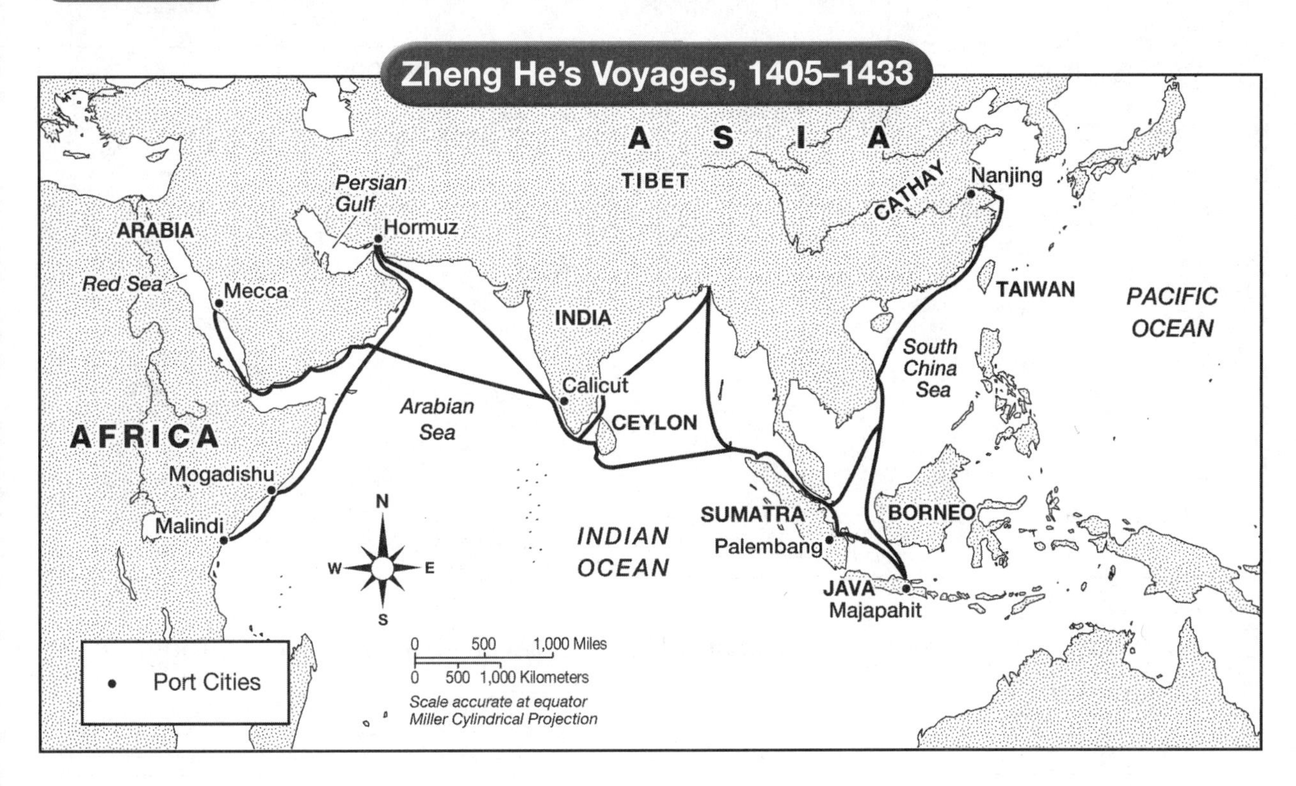

1. In what country is Calicut located? ______________________

2. Zheng He started his voyages in Cathay, or China. In which directions did he travel to reach Hormuz? ______________________

3. In what direction did Zheng He travel to get from Hormuz to Mogadishu?

____

4. What city in Arabia did Zheng He visit? ______________________

Name ______________________________ Date ______________

Background to European Exploration

Directions **Use the map and key to help you answer the questions. Write your answers in the blanks provided.**

The Silk Road

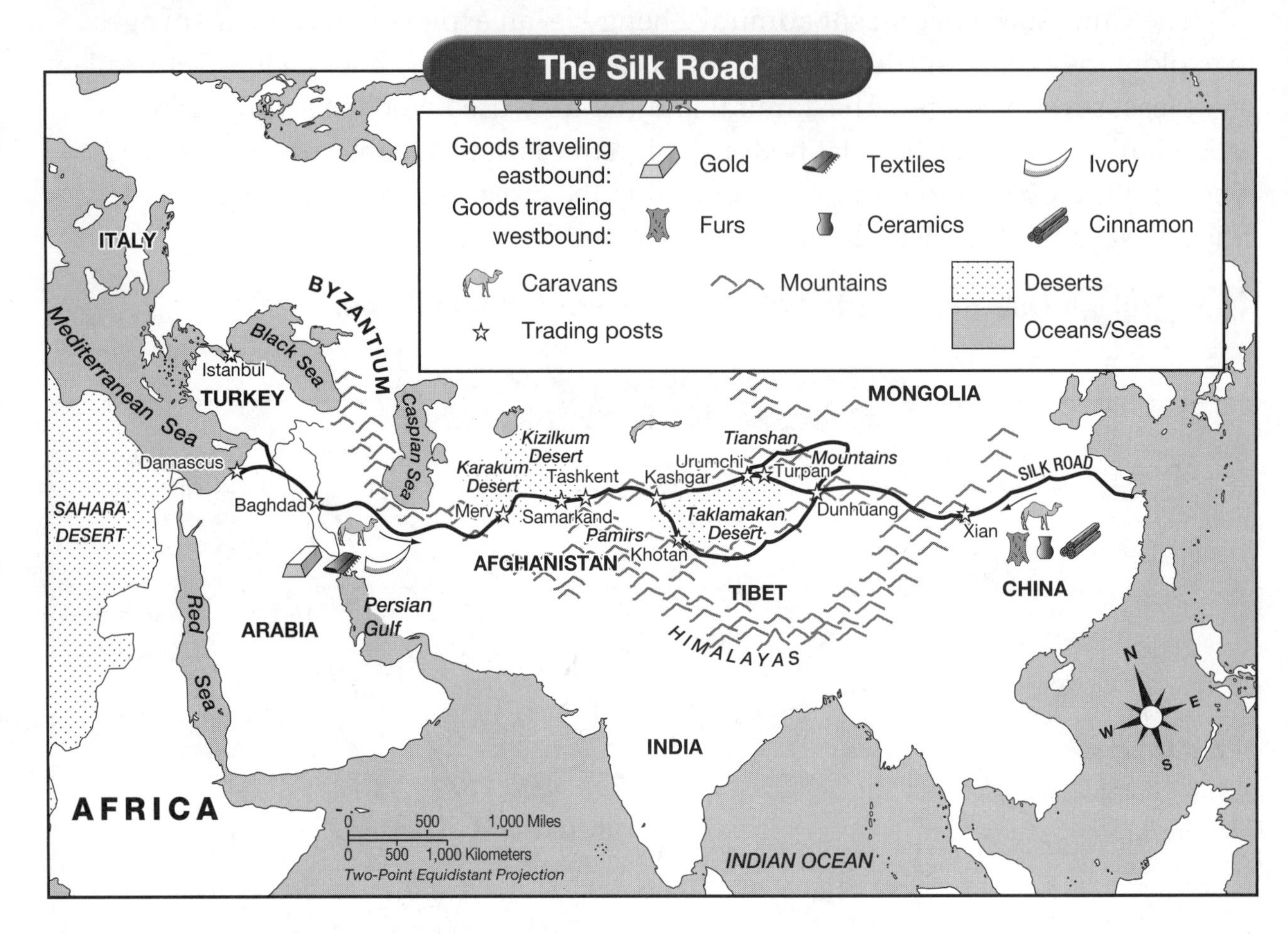

1. What are three kinds of goods transported by caravans traveling west through the Taklamakan Desert?

______________________, ______________________, ______________________

2. What three kinds of terrain would a caravan cross when traveling from Istanbul to Xian?

______________________, ______________________, ______________________

3. What three deserts are along the Silk Road?

______________________, ______________________, ______________________

Use after reading Chapter 3, Lesson 2, pages 114–119.

Name ______________________ Date ____________

READING SKILLS

Identify Causes and Their Effects

Directions **Write the cause for each effect in the box provided.**

Emperor Sunni Aui comes to power	development of the astrolabe	development of the caravel
invention of the compass	Turks capture Constantinople	cartographers begin working together
expeditions	Silk Road	

The compass—ancient and modern

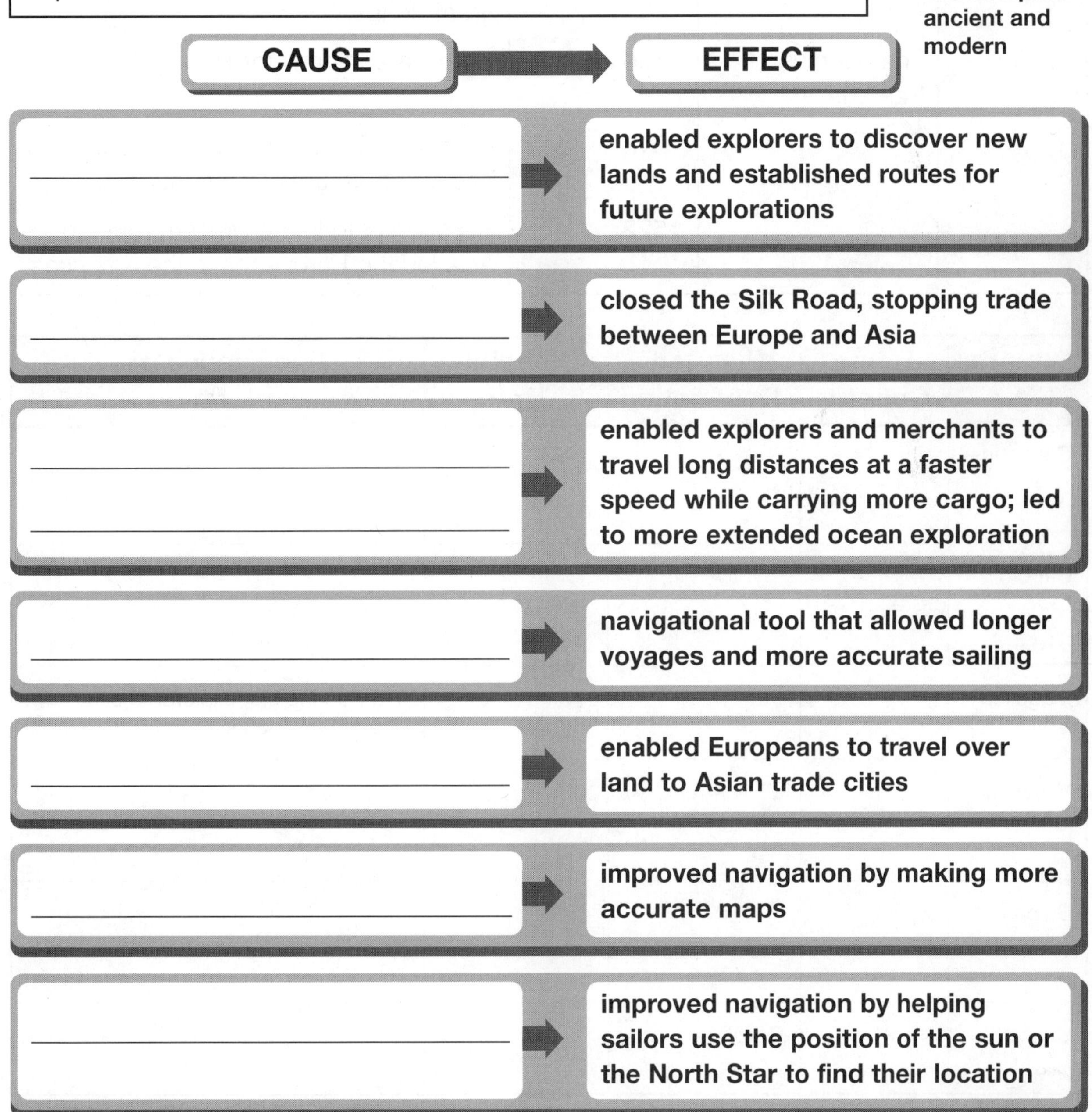

CAUSE	EFFECT
______________________	**enabled explorers to discover new lands and established routes for future explorations**
______________________	**closed the Silk Road, stopping trade between Europe and Asia**
______________________	**enabled explorers and merchants to travel long distances at a faster speed while carrying more cargo; led to more extended ocean exploration**
______________________	**navigational tool that allowed longer voyages and more accurate sailing**
______________________	**enabled Europeans to travel over land to Asian trade cities**
______________________	**improved navigation by making more accurate maps**
______________________	**improved navigation by helping sailors use the position of the sun or the North Star to find their location**

Use after reading Chapter 3, Skill Lesson, page 120.

Name ______________________ Date ______________

Europeans Reach the Americas

Columbus

Directions **Complete the chart using the information in the Word Bank. Some pieces of information may be used more than once.**

Home Country	Planned Destination	Expedition Date	Importance of Exploration
Italy	Asia	1497	He was the first explorer to prove Vespucci's idea.
Portugal	Cathay	1499	The king of England sent him to find great riches.
Spain	The Isthmus of Panama	1500	He claimed Brazil for Portugal.
		1513	He realized that he and other explorers had found an unknown continent.
		1522	His attempt to find a western route to Asia led the Europeans to the Americas.

Explorer	Home Country	Planned Destination	Expedition Date	Importance of Exploration
Columbus			1492	
Caboto				
Magellan				He was the first explorer to sail around the world.
Vespucci				
Balboa	Spain			
Cabral		Brazil		

Use after reading Chapter 3, Lesson 3, pages 121–126.

Name ______________________ Date ____________

The Spanish Conquerors

Directions **Write "T" or "F" in the blank before each statement to tell whether it is TRUE or FALSE. If the statement is FALSE, write the word that would make it TRUE in the blank at the end of the statement.**

Ponce de León

_____ 1 The English king offered grants of money to explorers who would lead expeditions. ____________

_____ 2 In 1513 Ponce de León set out to find Bimini and the "Fountain of Youth." ____________

_____ 3 Ponce de León claimed the land now known as Florida and named it *La Florida*, which is Spanish for "conquer." ____________

_____ 4 Cortés had heard stories about the great wealth of the Inca Empire. ____________

_____ 5 In 1519 Cortés traveled from the tropical coast to the Valley of Mexico, finally reaching Tenochtitlán. ____________

_____ 6 The French who were unhappy with Aztec rule gave the Spanish food and support against the Aztecs. ____________

_____ 7 The Aztec people believed that Cortés might be Quetzalcoatl. ____________

_____ 8 The survivors of Narváez's expedition sailed along the Pacific Coast until they reached Spanish lands in Mexico. ____________

_____ 9 Coronado and several Spaniards, Africans, and Native Americans set out to find the Seven Cities of Steel. ____________

_____ 10 In 1539 Hernando de Soto explored much of the North American Northwest. ____________

Use after reading Chapter 3, Lesson 4, pages 127–133.

Name ______________________________ Date ______________

Search for the Northwest Passage

Directions **Use the Word Bank below to complete the sentences.**

Arctic Ocean	Northwest Passage	estuary	*Half Moon*
gold	Iroquois	Dutch East India Company	*Dauphine*
King Francis I	Staten Island		Pamlico Sound

1. European explorers were looking for the ______________________, a waterway along the north coast of North America connecting the Atlantic Ocean and the Pacific Ocean.

2. In 1524 Giovanni da Verrazano set sail for North America on his ship, the ______________________.

Verrazano

3. A narrow body of water called the ______________________ lay between the Atlantic Ocean and what Verrazano thought was the Pacific Ocean.

4. Verrazano landed on the north end of present-day ______________________.

Cartier

5. ______________________ sent Jacques Cartier to North America to search for ______________________ and other valuable metals.

6. Cartier's ship sailed up the ______________________ of the St. Lawrence River.

7. During his expedition, Cartier was told by the ______________________ of jewels and metals that could be found northwest of Gaspe Peninsula.

8. Henry Hudson sailed by way of the ______________________ in search of the Northwest Passage.

9. The ______________________ gave Hudson a ship for his third voyage, his last attempt to find the Northwest Passage.

Hudson

10. Hudson's crew aboard the ______________________ mutinied in 1609.

Use after reading Chapter 3, Lesson 5, pages 136–139.

Name ______________________ Date ______________

European Exploration

Directions **Complete this graphic organizer to show that you understand the causes and effects of some of the key events that encouraged exploration and led to the discovery of the Americas.**

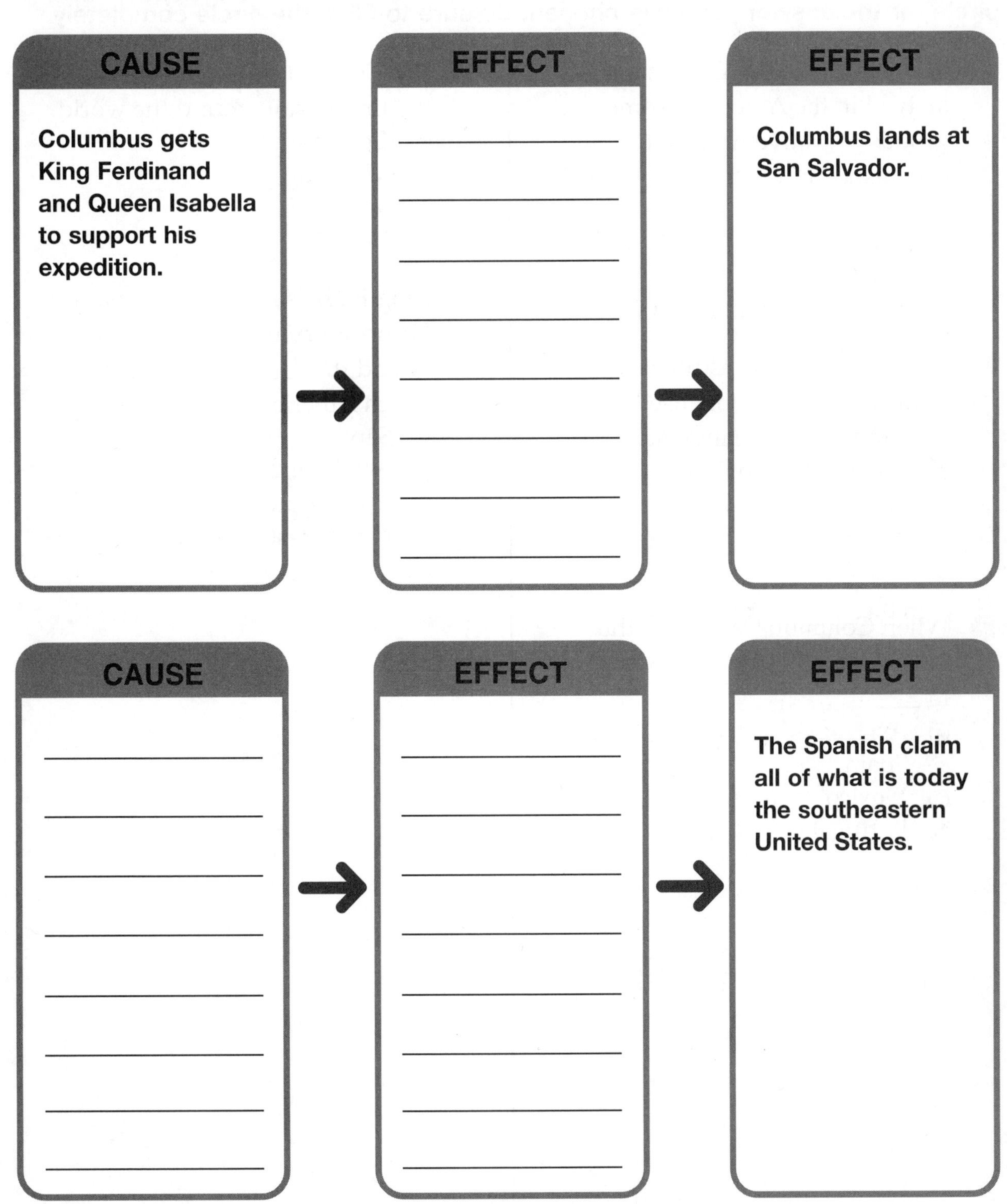

• CHAPTER •

3

Name ______________________ Date ______________

Test Preparation

Directions **Read each question and choose the best answer. Then fill in the circle for the answer you have chosen. Be sure to fill in the circle completely.**

1. Many years before Europeans arrived in the Americas, some groups of Native Americans had established powerful—
   - Ⓐ tribes.
   - Ⓑ fleets of ships.
   - Ⓒ empires.
   - Ⓓ trade agreements with China.

2. A compass and an astrolabe are kinds of ______ sailors used to determine their location at sea.
   - Ⓕ construction tools
   - Ⓖ navigational tools
   - Ⓗ books
   - Ⓙ telescopes

3. When Columbus landed in the Americas, he thought he was in ______.
   - Ⓐ Asia
   - Ⓑ Spain
   - Ⓒ Mexico
   - Ⓓ Portugal

4. The Portuguese explorer ______ was the first to sail around the world.
   - Ⓕ Columbus
   - Ⓖ Magellan
   - Ⓗ Vespucci
   - Ⓙ Cabral

5. King Francis I was one of many European rulers who wanted to find the ______ through North America.
   - Ⓐ Santa Fe Trail
   - Ⓑ Silk Road
   - Ⓒ trade route
   - Ⓓ Northwest Passage

Use after reading Chapter 3, pages 106–139.

Name ______________________________ Date ______________

New Spain

Directions **Write the number of the sentence under the appropriate heading in the Venn diagram.**

Before Spanish Colonies Established	Before and After	After Spanish Colonies Established

1. Many Native Americans died from a disease called smallpox.
2. The Plains Indians tamed horses and used them for hunting.
3. Native Americans were free from European diseases.
4. Gold, silver, and other treasures could be found in North America.
5. Native American tribes living in the borderlands traded with the Spanish.
6. The Navajos raised sheep and wove the wool into colorful clothing and blankets.
7. People could not travel on the *El Camino Real.*
8. Many Native Americans lived as free peoples in what is today known as Mexico.
9. Many Native Americans followed their traditional religions.
10. Missionaries persuaded some Native Americans to become Catholics.

Name ______________________ Date ______________

New France

Directions **Fill in the missing information in this letter from a member of Louis Joliet's crew. Use the words below to help you complete the letter.**

Jacques Marquette	Lake Michigan	Indian	canoes	1673
Northwest Passage	Mississippi	Spanish	languages	south

Dear Family:

In this year of ______________, I think of you often. I have set out with Joliet's crew on an expedition to find a great river called the ______________. We are traveling with a missionary named ______________ who speaks many Indian ______________.

We started our journey from northern ______________ in birch-bark ______________. We crossed a huge lake and several rivers. At last we saw the great Mississippi! Unfortunately, we realized it was not the ______________ that we were looking for because it flows ______________.

When we reached the mouth of the Arkansas River, we met some ______________ people who told us of Europeans living farther south along the river. We think those Europeans might be the ______________. We fear they may attack us, so we have decided to turn back.

I will think of you all as I journey home.

Sincerely,
François

Use after reading Chapter 4, Lesson 2, pages 150–155.

Name ______________________ Date ____________

The English in the Americas

Directions **Some of these sentences are causes, and some are effects. Complete the chart to show each cause and its effect.**

"Sea dogs" like Francis Drake become pirates.	England decides to start colonies in America.
Treasure captured by "sea dogs" helps increase England's wealth.	The English colonists at Roanoke Island arrive too late in the year to plant crops.

CAUSE	EFFECT
Elizabeth I encourages English sea captains to attack Spanish treasure ships.	______________________
______________________	England builds a strong navy with that wealth and becomes a powerful country.
Europe's most powerful countries have colonies in America.	______________________
______________________	John White returns to England to gather food and supplies.

Name ______________________ Date ______________

The Jamestown Colony

Directions **Use the chart below to answer the questions that follow.**

House of Burgesses			
Who?	**What?**	**When or Where?**	**How?**
Each Virginia settlement or plantation was allowed to elect two burgesses, usually wealthy landowners.	Virginia's legislature, the branch of the government that makes laws	Established July 30, 1619	Burgesses would meet once a year with the royal governor.
The 22 original burgesses were members of the House of Burgesses.	The first lawmaking assembly formed in the English colonies	Jamestown Colony	Burgesses and royal governor would meet to make local laws and decide on taxes.
Royal Governor George Yeardley shared ruling authority with the House of Burgesses.	Jamestown Colony would live under English law and have the same rights as the people living in England.	Met in the Jamestown church	Modeled after the English Parliament

1. What did the House of Burgesses do? ______________________

____

2. What country ruled Jamestown? ______________________

3. Who was the royal governor? ______________________

4. How often did the royal governor meet with the burgesses?

____

5. What governing body was the House of Burgesses modeled after?

____

6. When was the House of Burgesses established? ______________________

7. How did the burgesses decide on laws and taxes? ______________________

____

8. How many burgesses could be elected from each plantation or settlement?

____

Use after reading Chapter 4, Lesson 4, pages 160–164.

Name ______________________ Date ____________

CITIZENSHIP SKILLS

Solve a Problem

Directions **One problem in colonial times was that of getting settlers to stay for long periods of time. Imagine that you are a leader who wants to settle a colony. Use the steps below to complete the boxes and help you solve the problem. Step 1 has been done for you.**

Here are some questions to think about when solving your problem:

Where will the colonists live? How will they get food? How will they make a living? How will they prepare for winter? Who will govern the settlements? How will they respond to conflicts with other people?

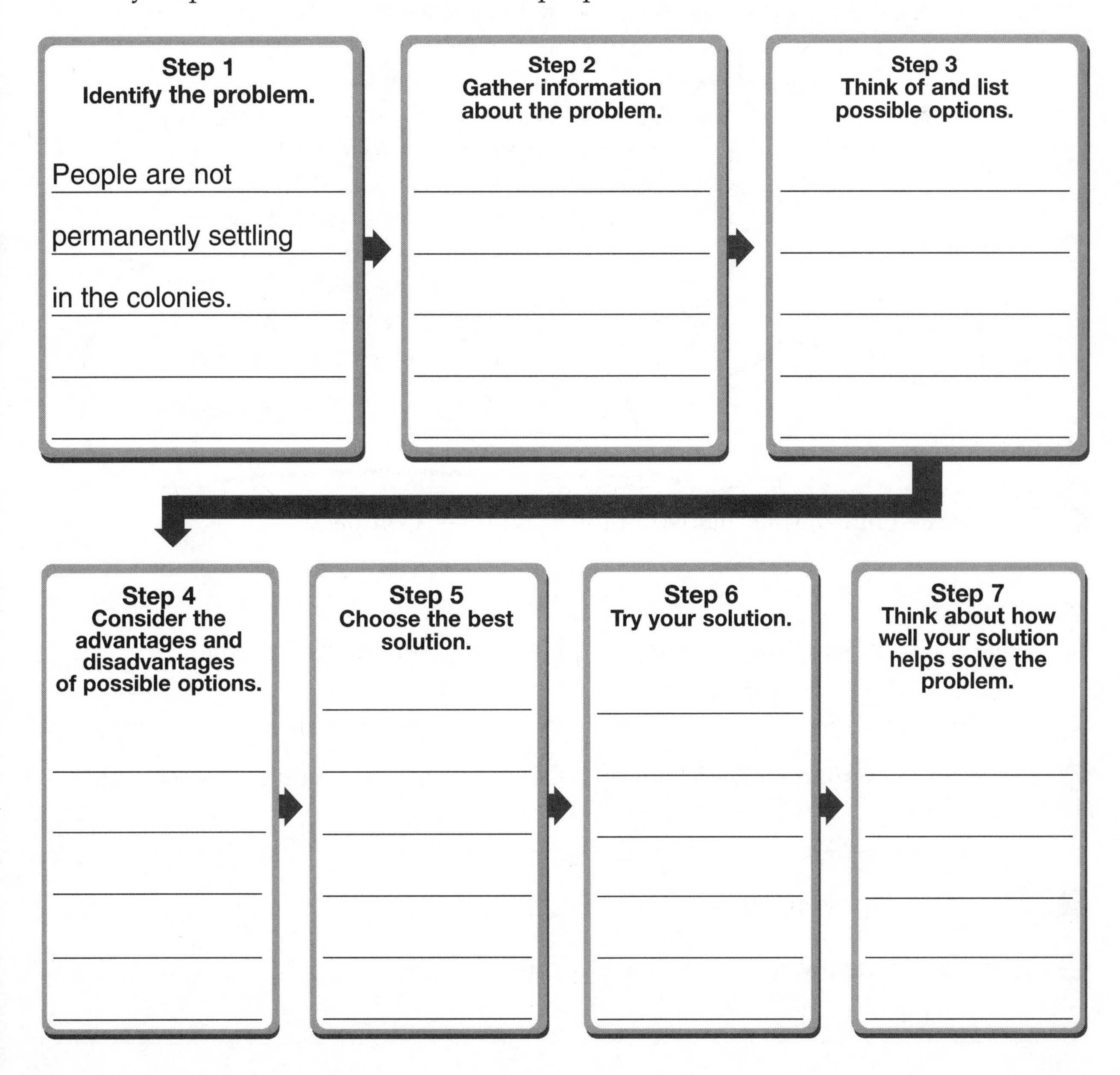

Use after reading Chapter 4, Skill Lesson, page 165.

Name ______________________ Date ____________

The Mayflower Compact

Directions **When the Mayflower Compact was written in 1620, the English language was very different from what it is today. Below is a version of the Mayflower Compact written in present-day language. Use it to answer the questions that follow.**

The Mayflower Compact

In the name of God, Amen. We, the loyal subjects of King James and the people of God have taken a voyage to settle in the first colony in the northern parts of Virginia. We, the people whose names are signed below, have made an agreement, in the presence of God and one another, to establish our own government of fair and equal laws. These laws will be decided by the majority rule of this group. These laws are made for the good of the people in the colony as well as for the colony itself. We promise to obey the laws we have made. We have signed our names below, at Cape Cod, on November 11, 1620.

Myles Standish William Bradford

1. Who is the English ruler named in the Mayflower Compact?

____

2. Where did the Mayflower passengers think they were going to settle?

____

3. How did the writers of the Mayflower Compact say laws would be decided?

____

4. What did the passengers promise? ______________________________

5. Where and when was the Mayflower Compact signed? ______________________________

____

Use after reading Chapter 4, Lesson 5, pages 166–170.

Name ______________________ Date ______________

CHART AND GRAPH SKILLS

Compare Tables to Classify Information

Directions **Read and study each table. Use the information in the tables to answer the questions below.**

Table A: Native Americans and European Colonists

Colony	Native American Tribe Encountered	Interaction/Events
Connecticut (1636)	Pequot	Colonists purchased land; later, tribe fought to reclaim land.
New Jersey (1664)	Lenape	Colonists fought with this hostile tribe.
New York (1626)	Algonquian-speaking tribes	Colonists bought Manhattan Island from local tribes.
Rhode Island (1636)	Algonquian-speaking tribes, mostly Narragansett	Colonists peacefully coexisted with local tribes.

Table B: Native Americans and European Colonists

Interaction/Events	Native American Tribe Encountered	Colony
Colonists bought Manhattan Island from local tribes.	Algonquian-speaking tribes	New York (1626)
Colonists purchased land; later, tribe fought to reclaim land.	Pequot	Connecticut (1636)
Colonists peacefully coexisted with local tribes.	Algonquian-speaking tribes, mostly Narragansett	Rhode Island (1636)
Colonists fought with this hostile tribe.	Lenape	New Jersey (1664)

1. Which table makes it easier to find out when the first colony was established?

   Why? ______________________

2. Which table would you use to find which colony bought an island from Native Americans? Why? ______________________

3. Which table would you use to find out which Native American tribe was found in New Jersey? Why? ______________________

Name ______________________ Date ______________

Key Settlements in North America

Directions **Complete this graphic organizer by categorizing people and settlements with the country they are associated with.**

SPANISH SETTLEMENTS	FRENCH SETTLEMENTS	ENGLISH SETTLEMENTS

KEY PEOPLE	**KEY PEOPLE**	**KEY PEOPLE**
1. Bartolomé de Las Casas	1. Samuel de Champlain	1. Sir Francis Drake
2.	2.	2.
3.	3.	3.
KEY SETTLEMENTS	**KEY SETTLEMENTS**	**KEY SETTLEMENTS**
1. Hispaniola	1. Quebec	1. Roanoke
2.	2.	2.
3.	3.	3.

Use after reading Chapter 4, pages 143–171.

Name ______________________ Date ____________

Test Preparation

Directions **Read each question and choose the best answer. Then fill in the circle for the answer you have chosen. Be sure to fill in the circle completely.**

1. What did the Spanish create in North America to protect their colonies from other Europeans?
   - Ⓐ a hacienda
   - Ⓑ a buffer zone
   - Ⓒ a mission
   - Ⓓ a ranch

2. What was the main item of trade between the French and the Native Americans in New France?
   - Ⓕ fur
   - Ⓖ gold
   - Ⓗ silk
   - Ⓙ food

3. Who protected the English "sea dogs" when they stole treasures from the Spanish?
   - Ⓐ Native Americans
   - Ⓑ the French
   - Ⓒ the queen of England
   - Ⓓ conquistadors

4. What is a burgess?
   - Ⓕ a representative
   - Ⓖ a royal governor
   - Ⓗ a company
   - Ⓙ a monarchy

5. Why did the Pilgrims sail to North America in 1620?
   - Ⓐ to meet Native Americans
   - Ⓑ to practice their religion in their own way
   - Ⓒ to be farmers
   - Ⓓ to trade fur

Use after reading Chapter 4, pages 144–171.

Name ______________________________ Date ______________

Massachusetts Bay Colony

Directions **Find the terms in the Word Bank in the Word Search Puzzle. Words may be arranged vertically, horizontally, or diagonally.**

Puritan	charter	common	specialize	town meeting
public office	blacksmith	churn	colony	confederation
school	constable	kettle	patchwork quilts	candles
livestock	soap	crops	preserved	pickled vegetables

y s d e h c s o o c v d c a n d l e s b q z s d f w q

h k o f d e s n a h r t e d f h j c c o l o n y u b t

n r v y q w p p r e s e r v e d a o y k a n b m k g b

y t r d c t d e a m c b n t i u u d h p c p x v c s l

t j u u o r d c e t o w n m e e t i n g a u a k r f a

n m t l n o l u p i c k l e d v e g e t a b l e s q c

k g f t s e d t u y h h j k g o y t g b j l s f d a k

d e i b t u y t r c a x w l k u j h v y u i c z i x s

c r t v a b c n i l r v c o m m o n y a o c r m x u m

b t f t b j h k t v t x h d r l k i j d c o k s d s i

i u f r l h z s a r e g u g m k g h r f y f e r p c t

w s b n e e k m n y r e r s d e q j f w d f j o d h h

o l p u h j f r t d o k n f d e t u i u y i r x c o m

w d e s s p e c i a l i z e t f h y i r e c i u k o p

u e h s g a i w k e d j o l h j i k g l t e c w o l n

k l n f l i v e s t o c k d a s j w e h t a g n c b d

m f d j s e i c o n f e d e r a t i o n k s s a e l s

(continued)

Use after reading Chapter 5, Lesson 1, pages 188–193.

Name ______________________________ Date ______________

Directions **Use words from the word bank on the previous page to complete the sentences below.**

1. In 1628 King Charles I granted a ______________________________, to a group of Puritans, allowing them to settle in New England.

2. John Winthrop served as governor in one ______________________________ several times during a 20-year period.

3. Winthrop formed a ______________________________ among the people of New England so they could better defend themselves against their enemies.

4. A place for the town animals to graze was one use for the ______________________________.

5. A ______________________________ specialized in working with iron.

6. A law was passed stating that any town with more than 50 families must have a ______________________________.

7. Both men and women could attend a ______________________________, but only the men could vote.

8. One public official was a ______________________________, who was in charge of maintaining order and keeping the peace.

9. ______________________________ could be stored and eaten throughout the winter.

10. Some food, as well as leather and wool, came from farmers' ______________________________.

Name ______________________ Date ____________

New Ideas, New Colonies

Directions **Complete the information in the boxes next to the map. Use the names and terms below to help you.**

Thomas Hooker	Roger Williams	consent
John Endecott	Fundamental Orders	self-governed by Puritan leaders

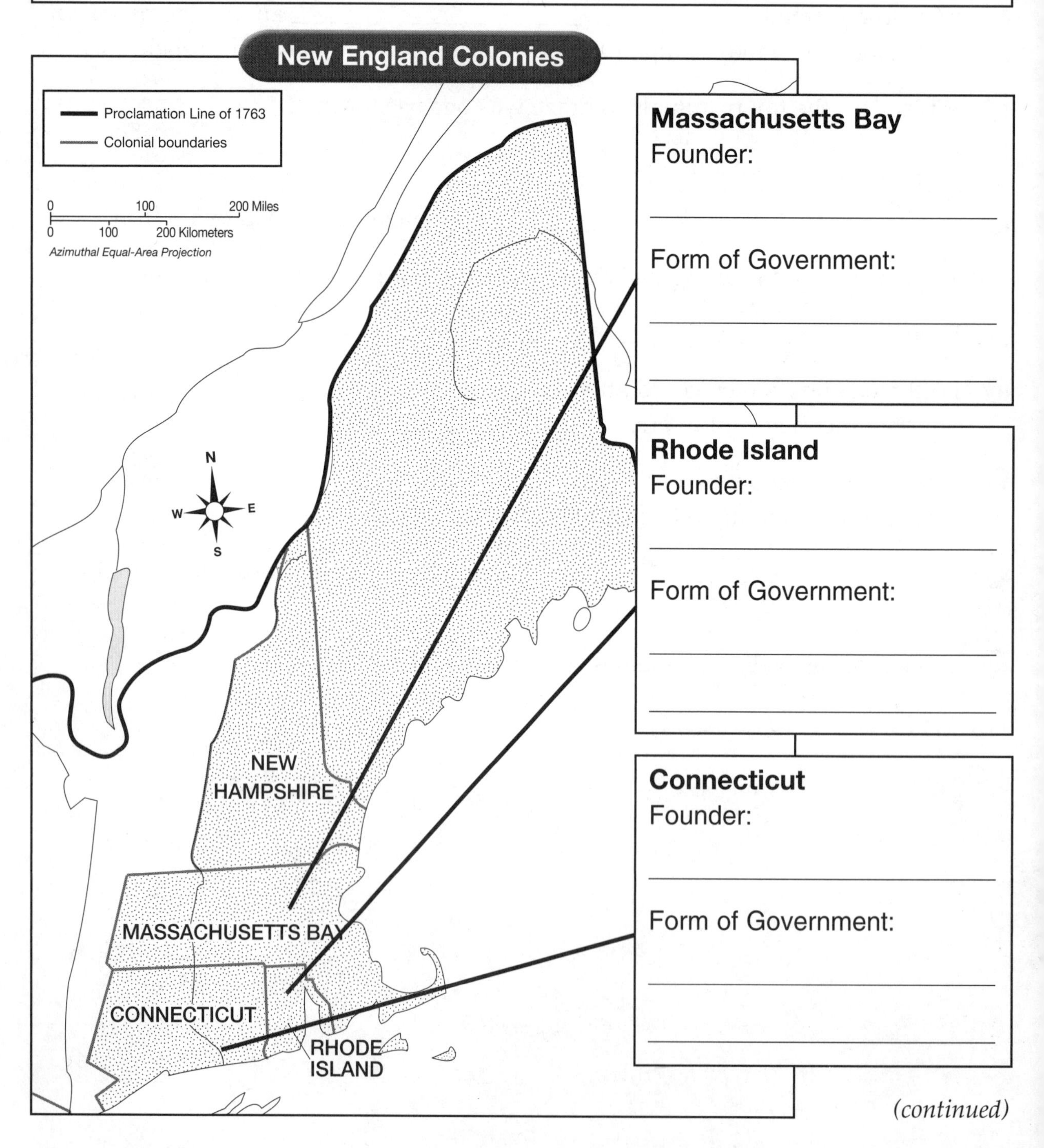

(continued)

Use after reading Chapter 5, Lesson 2, pages 194–199.

Name ______________________ Date ____________

Directions **Use the map on the previous page and the words and sentences below to help you complete the table and answer the questions.**

Places, Tribes, and Dates:	**Events:**
1636	Expelled from the colony, Williams moved his family to Narragansett Bay.
Narragansett	Puritans disagreed with practices of the Church of England.
Windsor, 1633	
Providence, 1636	

Founded	**Massachusetts Bay Colony**	**Rhode Island Colony**	**Connecticut Colony**
When	1628	____________	1630s
Why	____________ ____________ ____________ ____________	____________ ____________ ____________ ____________	Some colonists were looking for better farmland; other colonists wanted religious freedom.
Where	Salem, 1628	____________	____________
Which tribe was there?	Wampanoags	____________	Pequots

1. When was the Connecticut Colony founded? ____________

2. What was the major event that led to the founding of the Massachusetts Bay Colony? ____________

3. What Native American tribe did the Massachusetts Bay Colony interact with?

____

4. Who moved to Narragansett Bay? ____________

Name ____________________ Date ____________

New England's Economy

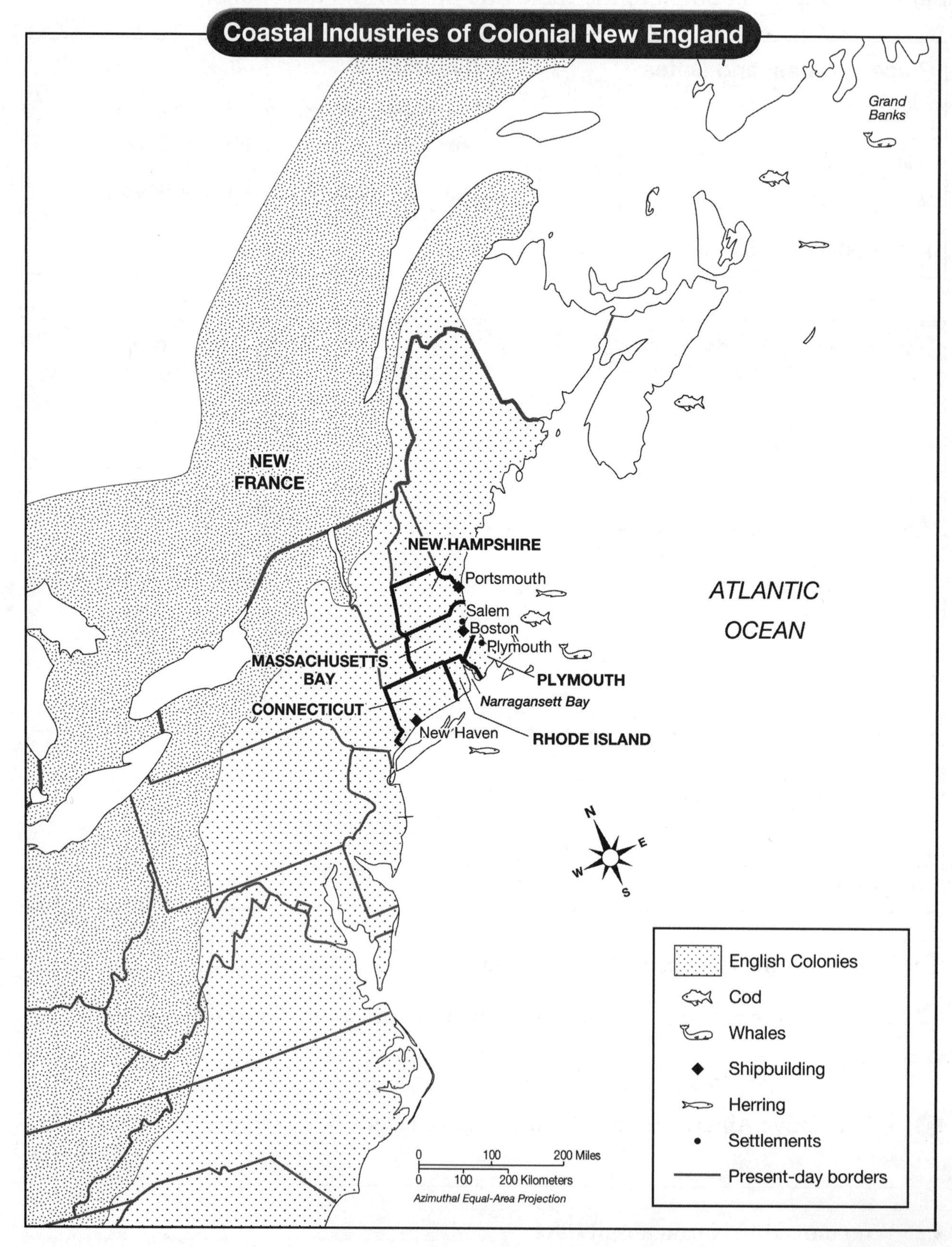

(continued)

Use after reading Chapter 5, Lesson 3, pages 200–204.

Name ______________________ Date ____________

Directions **Use the map on page 48 to help you answer some of the questions below.**

1. Shade in the area that shows the New England Colonies.

2. Other than the English colonies, what land area was near the Grand Banks?

   ____

3. In what three settlements and colonies were the shipbuilding centers located?

   ____

   ____

4. What were two locations where whales were caught? ______________________

   ____

5. In what ocean did the colonists fish? ______________________

6. What important product came from whales, and what was it used for?

   ____

7. When whalers first began hunting, they used small rowboats and were able to find many whales near the shore. Later, the whalers needed bigger ships, and their whaling trips lasted much longer. Sometimes, whalers were gone for many months or even years. Explain why the whaling industry changed.

   ____

   ____

   ____

8. Why did shipbuilders choose coastal locations such as Portsmouth for shipbuilding? ______________________

   ____

   ____

Name ______________________________ Date ______________

CHART AND GRAPH SKILLS

Read a Line Graph

Directions **Study the line graph below. Use it to help you determine whether the statements on page 51 are true or false.**

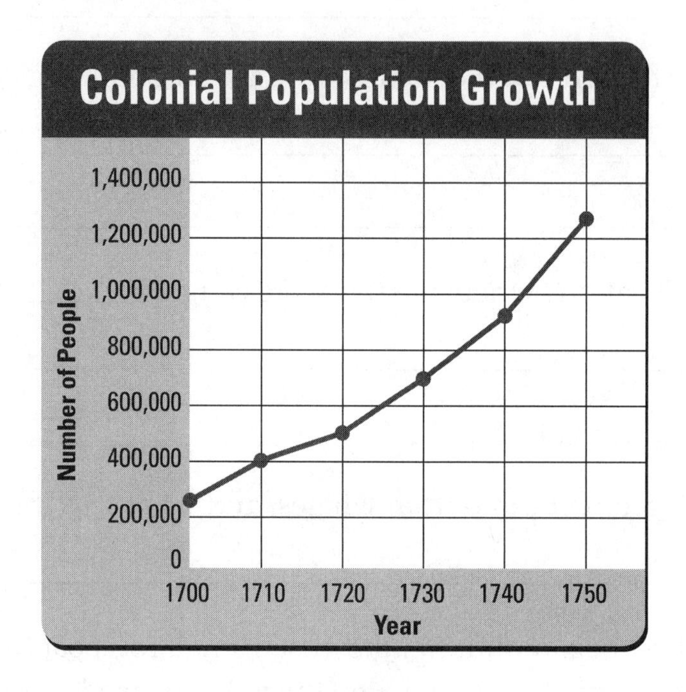

Directions **Circle *T* if the sentence is true. Circle *F* if the sentence is false.**

1. There were more than 2 million people in the colonies by 1750. T F
2. The population growth was less than 500,000 between 1700 and 1710. T F
3. There were nearly twice as many people in 1740 as there were in 1720. T F
4. One of the largest population increases occurred between 1720 and 1730. T F

(continued)

Use after reading Chapter 5, Skill Lesson, page 205.

Name ______________________________ Date ______________

5. The population was almost a million people in 1740. T F

6. Given the growth of the population between 1740 and 1750, what would the projected population be for 1760? Read the graph, and list the numbers for each point on the graph.

1740 ______________________________

1750 ______________________________

1760 ______________________________

7. By the early 1700s the colonies were well established and colonists were relatively healthy. Many colonists had large families—sometimes with ten or more children. In addition, new settlers continued to arrive. Using the line graph, explain the effect that these factors had on the population of the colonies.

____

____

____

Name ______________________________ Date ______________

The Massachusetts Bay Colony

Directions **Complete this graphic organizer by summarizing the following facts about the Massachusetts Bay Colony.**

FACTS		SUMMARY
1. The Puritans built many villages in North America. 2. The most important building in a Puritan village was the meetinghouse. 3. The village meetinghouse served as a church and a place to hold town meetings.		______________________________
1. Roger Williams was forced to leave the Massachusetts Bay Colony. 2. Anne Hutchinson was also forced to leave the colony. 3. Roger Williams and Anne Hutchinson and their followers established their own settlements.		______________________________
1. Trading goods made many people wealthy in New England. 2. Goods were traded between the colonies, England, and the west coast of Africa. 3. Trade brought the first African slaves to the English Colonies.		______________________________

Use after reading Chapter 5, pages 187–205.

Name ______________________ Date ______________

Test Preparation

Directions **Read each question and choose the best answer. Then fill in the circle for the answer you have chosen. Be sure to fill in the circle completely.**

1. Which group of people settled in New England because they disagreed with many practices of the Church of England?
   - Ⓐ colonists
   - Ⓑ settlers
   - Ⓒ Puritans
   - Ⓓ Christians

2. Who had a conflict with the Puritan leaders in the Massachusetts Bay Colony?
   - Ⓕ Anne Hutchinson
   - Ⓖ Roger Williams
   - Ⓗ both F and G
   - Ⓙ John Winthrop

3. Where did some colonists go to find better farmland?
   - Ⓐ Rhode Island
   - Ⓑ Connecticut
   - Ⓒ Massachusetts Bay
   - Ⓓ Plymouth

4. Why was whale oil a popular product?
   - Ⓕ It burned brightly without an unpleasant odor.
   - Ⓖ It was very inexpensive.
   - Ⓗ It was available in unlimited quantities.
   - Ⓙ both G and H

5. ______ were workers who used wood to make barrels and casks.
   - Ⓐ Merchants
   - Ⓑ Shipbuilders
   - Ⓒ Fishermen
   - Ⓓ Coopers

Name ______________________ Date ______________

Breadbasket Colonies

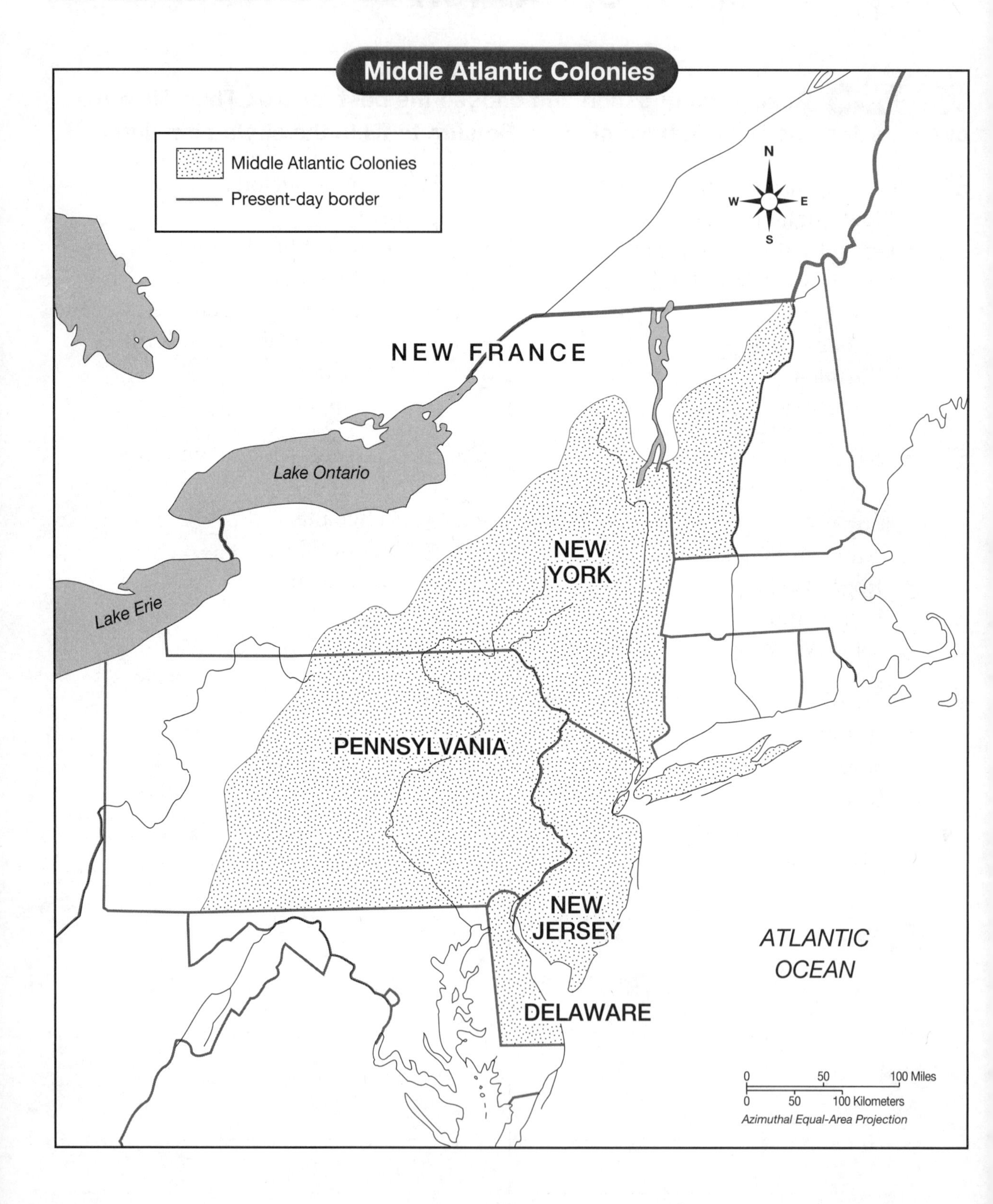

(continued)

Use after reading Chapter 6, Lesson 1, pages 210–215.

Name ______________________ Date ____________

Directions **Read each lettered phrase below. On the map, write the letter of the phrase in the colony or colonies to which it applies.**

A. settled by Quakers

B. bought from the Manhattan Indians by Peter Minuit

C. freedom of speech, freedom of worship, and trial by jury

D. William Penn

E. John Berkeley and George Carteret

F. colonists fought Delaware and Wappinger Indians

G. Peter Stuyvesant

H. "Penn's woods"

I. Native American Chief Tamenend

J. claimed for Holland by Henry Hudson

K. Fort Christina

L. Edward Byllinge

Why were the Middle Atlantic Colonies called the "breadbasket colonies"?

____

____

____

____

____

____

____

____

____

____

Name ______________________ Date ____________

Colonial Philadelphia

Benjamin Franklin

William Penn

Facts About William Penn and Benjamin Franklin

Founded Philadelphia on the idea that people of different backgrounds could live in peace together

Wrote "Early to bed and early to rise makes a man healthy, wealthy, and wise"

Designed the layout of Philadelphia, with a "checkerboard" plan for the center

Printed a newspaper called the *Pennsylvania Gazette*

Organized the first firefighting company in the colonies

Named his colony's chief city Philadelphia

Worked to have Philadelphia's streets lit at night and paved

Divided his colony into townships made up of 5,000 acres each

Helped establish the first subscription library

Added public parks to the city he called "a green country town"

Planned the government and the settlements of Philadelphia

Invented the lightning rod, which helped protect buildings from lightning

(continued)

Use after reading Chapter 6, Lesson 2, pages 218–222.

Name ______________________ Date ____________

Directions **Read the facts about William Penn and Benjamin Franklin on page 56. Decide which facts describe each person. Then use the facts to fill in the table below.**

William Penn	Benjamin Franklin

Name ______________________ Date ____________

CHART AND GRAPH SKILLS

Use a Circle Graph

Directions **Use the circle graph to help you answer the questions below.**

Population of the 13 Colonies, 1750

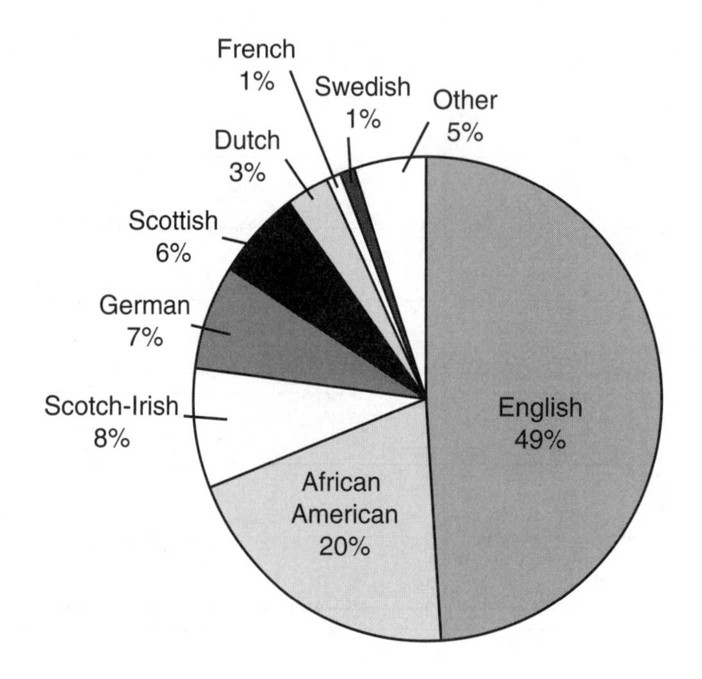

1. What was the largest ethnic group in the 13 colonies in 1750?

 ____

2. What were the smallest ethnic groups? ______________________

3. Which group was larger, German or Scottish? ______________________

4. What percent of the population was African American? ______________________

5. What was the combined percent of African American and English people?

 ____

6. What was the combined percent of all non-English people?

 ____

(continued)

Use after reading Chapter 6, Skill Lesson, page 223.

Name ______________________ Date ____________

Directions **Use the table to help you complete the activities.**

In addition to Quaker meetinghouses, there were many kinds of churches in Pennsylvania. Use the information in the table to make a circle graph of the kinds of churches in Pennsylvania other than Quaker meetinghouses.

Pennsylvania Churches* in 1750	
Church	**Percent of Population**
Dutch Reformed	32%
Lutheran	28%
Baptist	15%
Anglican	10%
German Reformed	6%
Catholic	6%
Congregationalist	3%

*Quaker meetinghouses not included

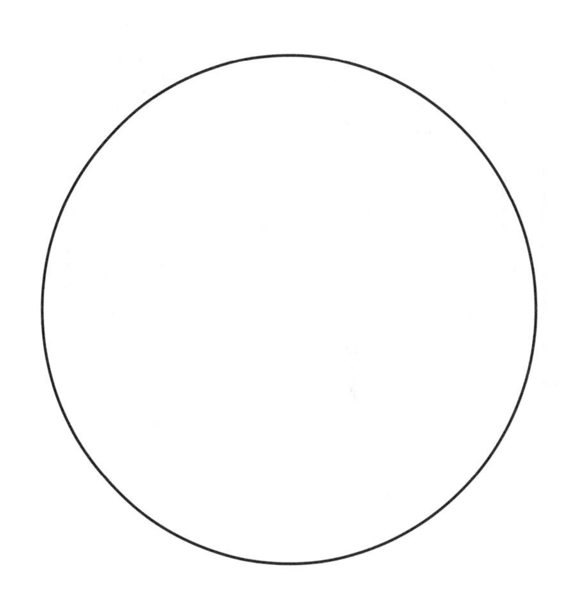

Use the information from the circle graph you have made to write a paragraph about church memberships in Pennsylvania. Be sure to discuss why you think Pennsylvania had so many different kinds of churches.

____

____

____

____

____

____

____

____

____

Use after reading Chapter 6, Skill Lesson, page 223.

Name ______________________ Date ______________

Moving West

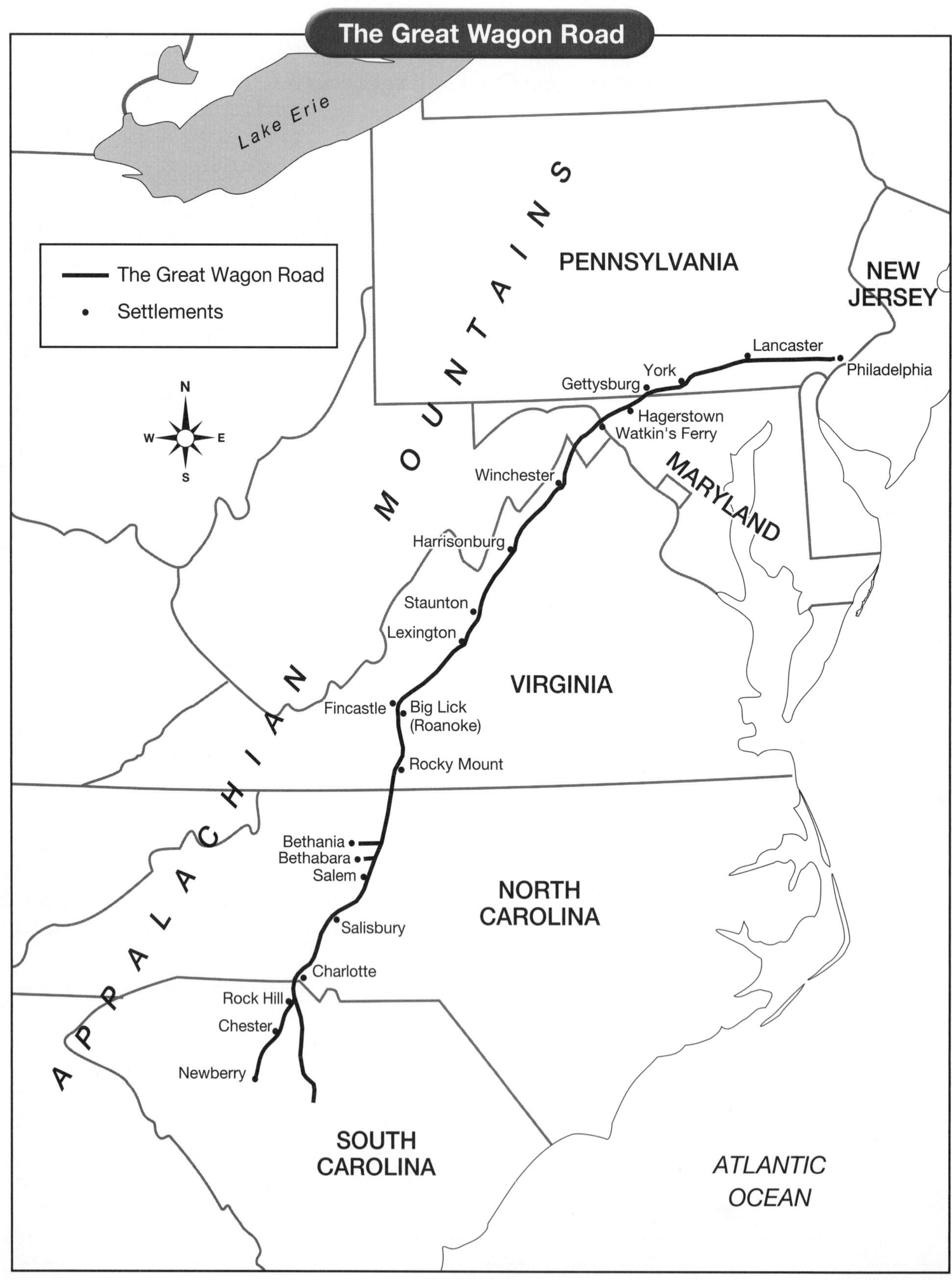

(continued)

Use after reading Chapter 6, Lesson 3, pages 224–227.

Name ______________________ Date ____________

Directions **Read the paragraph below and use the map on the previous page to label the sentences. If the sentence is true, write *T* in the blank provided. If it is false, write *F*.**

Traveling on the Great Wagon Road

The Great Wagon Road extended from Pennsylvania to South Carolina. Travel along the hilly route was difficult, and journeys lasted at least two months. Even the fastest wagon traveled only five miles a day. Often people crossed rivers by wading through them while guiding their wagons or carrying supplies. Although the weather was harsh, people frequently made the trip in winter because it was easier to travel on the frozen roads. Each year the Great Wagon Road stretched farther south, so that by 1775 it was close to 600 miles long. In the decade before the American Revolution, tens of thousands of settlers journeyed down the road in search of new opportunities. During this time, the Great Wagon Road was the most heavily traveled road in the colonies.

1. ______ Settlements along the Great Wagon Road included York, Harrisonburg, Salisbury, and New York City.
2. ______ Salisbury is located on the east side of the Great Wagon Road in North Carolina.
3. ______ People frequently journeyed along the Great Wagon Road in the winter because it was easier to travel on the frozen roads.
4. ______ The Great Wagon Road ran through parts of five different colonies.
5. ______ The fastest wagons journeying on the Great Wagon Road traveled 25 miles a day.
6. Compare and contrast travel on American highways today with travel along the Great Wagon Road in the mid-1700s. ______________________

____

____

____

____

____

Name ______________________ Date ______________

Chapter Review

Directions **Complete this graphic organizer by using information you have learned from the chapter to make inferences about the Middle Atlantic Colonies and the backcountry.**

Breadbasket Colonies

WHAT YOU HAVE READ	WHAT YOU KNOW
The Middle Atlantic Colonies attracted people from many different backgrounds.	______________

____

Moving West

WHAT YOU HAVE READ	WHAT YOU KNOW
Colonists who settled land farther west faced many challenges.	______________

____

Use after reading Chapter 6, pages 208–227.

Name ________________ Date ________

6 Test Preparation

Directions **Read each question and choose the best answer. Then fill in the circle for the answer you have chosen. Be sure to fill in the circle completely.**

1. Farmers depended on ______ as places to trade their surplus farm produce.
   - Ⓐ crops
   - Ⓑ agriculture
   - Ⓒ market towns
   - Ⓓ meetinghouses

2. Philadelphia's location near good land and ______ was one reason it became Pennsylvania's main port.
   - Ⓕ waterways
   - Ⓖ wagon roads
   - Ⓗ oceans
   - Ⓙ fertile soil

3. The English and the ______ who came with William Penn were the largest groups of immigrants in Philadelphia.
   - Ⓐ Puritans
   - Ⓑ Catholics
   - Ⓒ Quakers
   - Ⓓ Shakers

4. The land between the Coastal Plain and the Appalachian Mountains is called the—
   - Ⓕ farmland.
   - Ⓖ backcountry.
   - Ⓗ city.
   - Ⓙ Fall Line.

5. Backcountry family members all had to do jobs or chores, such as—
   - Ⓐ chopping wood.
   - Ⓑ hunting.
   - Ⓒ candle making.
   - Ⓓ all of the above.

Name ____________________ Date ____________

Settlement of the South

Directions **Use the Word Bank to provide the missing information in the chart.**

to make money from cash crops	Catholic landowners
the Lords Proprietors	James Oglethorpe
to give debtors a new start	French Huguenots
divided into two colonies	freedom to worship
1633	English

Settling the Southern Colonies

Where	Who	Why	When
Maryland	Founders: the Calverts, ____________ First proprietor: Cecilius Calvert First governor: Leonard Calvert	____________ ____________	____________
Carolina	First proprietors: ____________ (8 English nobles) First colonists: English settlers, settlers from the Caribbean, and ____________ First governor: William Drummond	____________ ____________ ____________	1663 1712: ____________ ____________ ____________
Georgia	First proprietors: ____________ and 19 partners First colonists: ____________	____________ ____________ ____________	1733

(continued)

Use after reading Chapter 7, Lesson 1, pages 232–239.

Name ______________________ Date ____________

Directions **Use the chart on the preceding page to help you write answers to the questions.**

1. Which colony wanted to help debtors? ______________________

2. What happened in Carolina in 1712? ______________________

____

3. Who were the Calverts? What colony did they found?

____

4. What freedom did the colonists of Maryland want? ______________________

____

5. Who were the Lords Proprietors, and what was their role in the colony?

____

6. From what country were the Huguenots? ______________________

7. What colony grew cash crops? Why do you think cash crops were important to the colonists? ______________________

____

____

Name ______________________________ Date ______________

READING SKILLS

Tell Fact From Opinion

Directions **Read the paragraph below. Use the information in the paragraph to identify each statement as Fact or Opinion. In the blanks, write *F* if the statement is a fact and write *O* if the statement is an opinion.**

James Oglethorpe

While a lawmaker in England, James Oglethorpe heard that a good friend had been sent to prison for not paying his debts. Oglethorpe hurried to the prison but arrived too late. His friend had died of smallpox. In memory of this friend, Oglethorpe decided to help debtors. One way he did this was by bringing debtors to the new colony of Georgia. Oglethorpe offered each settler a 50-acre bonus for every debtor that the settler brought along to help with the work of starting a colony. There the debtors could work for the settlers and pay back the money they owed. Oglethorpe hoped that debtors would work hard if they were given a second chance.

1. ______ James Oglethorpe was a lawmaker in England.
2. ______ A good friend of Oglethorpe's was in prison.
3. ______ Oglethorpe did not arrive in time to help his friend.
4. ______ Smallpox is the worst of all diseases.
5. ______ Oglethorpe decided to help debtors.
6. ______ Oglethorpe's idea to help debtors was a good one.
7. ______ Hard work would benefit the debtors.
8. ______ Debtors came to the Georgia Colony.
9. ______ Oglethorpe was a good man.

Use after reading Chapter 7, Skill Lesson, page 240.

Name ______________________ Date ______________

Southern Plantations

Directions **Read the sentences below and decide whether the information applies to slaves or indentured servants. Circle the letter under the appropriate column. Then write that letter in the appropriate blank below.**

	Plantation Workers	Slaves	Indentured Servants
1	Sent by the English courts to work in the colonies to pay for their crimes	S	W
2	Kidnapped and sold in the colonies	E	M
3	Came willingly to the English colonies	O	D
4	Sold like property at auctions	R	U
5	Were given their freedom after a certain length of time	H	A
6	Were punished by overseers if they did not work hard	T	C
7	Had little money to travel, so they went with others and worked off their debts	N	T
8	Two kinds of these workers existed: field and house	E	P
9	Were forbidden by law to learn how to read and write	I	J

Where were the earliest plantations usually built?

___	___	___	___	___	___	___	___	___
6	9	3	8	1	5	7	2	4

Name ______________________________ Date ______________

MAP AND GLOBE SKILLS

Read a Product Map

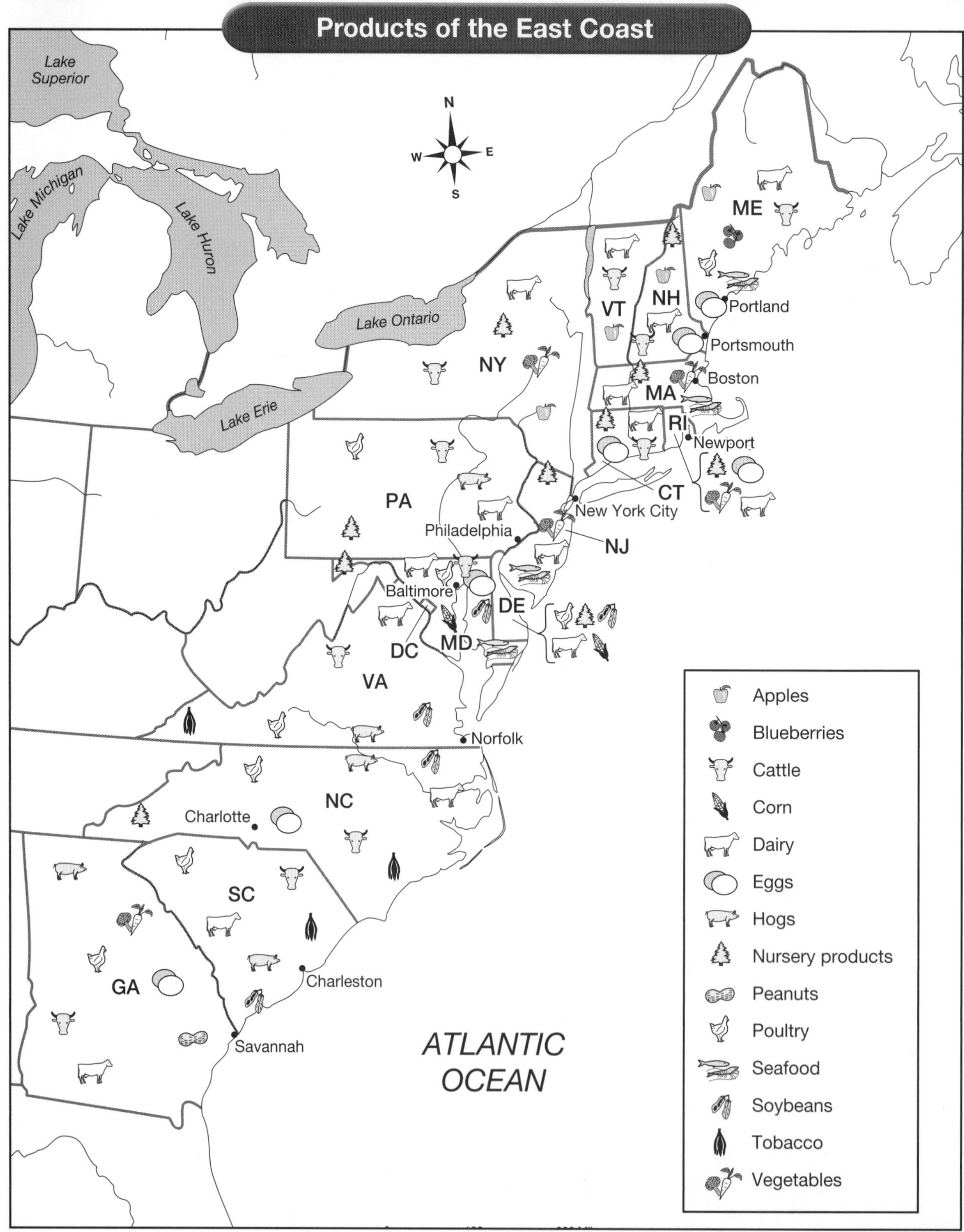

(continued)

Use after reading Chapter 7, Skill Lesson, pages 246–247.

Name ______________________ Date ____________

Directions **Use the map on page 68 to help you answer the questions.**

1. What product is produced in every state? ______________________

2. Where on the East Coast will you find tobacco grown? ______________________

____

3. In which state are blueberries grown? ______________________

4. Where on the East Coast will you find apples grown? ______________________

____

5. Where are soybeans grown? ______________________

____

6. Which two states grow exactly the same kinds of products?

____

____

7. In which state are peanuts grown? ______________________

8. What products are produced in South Carolina that are not produced in Maine?

____

Use the map to explain what opportunities there might be for a person looking for a job in the southern states.

____

____

____

____

____

____

____

____

Name ______________________________ Date ______________

Southern Cities

Directions **Fill in each blank with the correct word.**

1. Some workers specialized as fishers, tailors, printers, or ______________.

2. A young person often learned a trade by becoming an ______________.

3. ______________ and ______________ had the most power in Charles Town society.

4. What was one reason wealthy planters lived in Charles Town during the summer months? ______________________________

   ____

5. What did colonists find when they moved north along the Atlantic coast in search of fertile soil for plantations? What did they do with their find?

   ____

6. Some of Wilmington's earliest immigrants came from ______________

   ______________________________.

7. The Georgia Colony's chief port was the coastal town of ______________.

8. What were the three products that caused Norfolk, Virginia, to grow quickly?

   ____

9. In Baltimore the ______________ River flows into the

   ______________ Bay.

10. What was the reason for Baltimore's successful shipyards?

    ____

Use after reading Chapter 7, Lesson 3, pages 248–251.

Name ______________________________ Date ______________

The Southern Colonies

Directions **Complete this graphic organizer by using facts you have learned from the chapter to make generalizations about the Southern Colonies.**

1. Settlement of the South

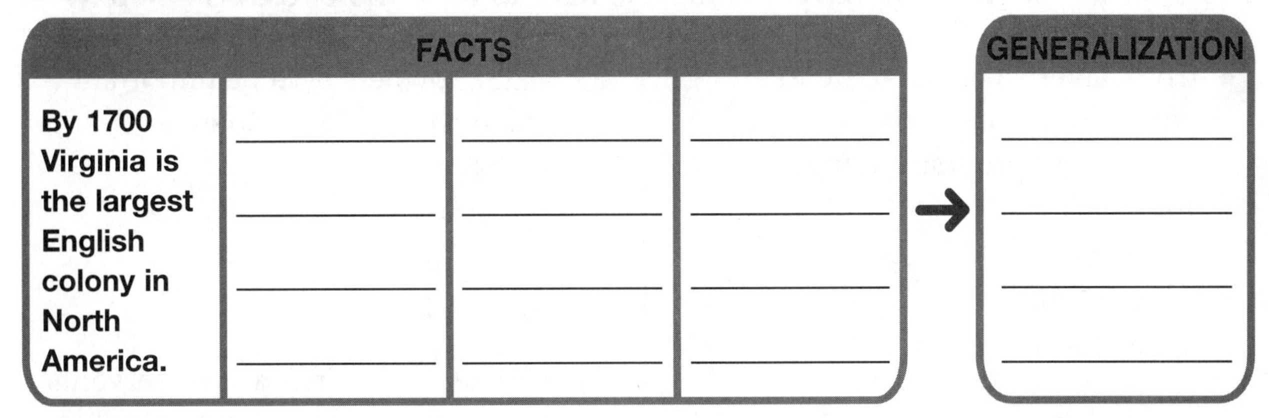

2. Southern Plantations

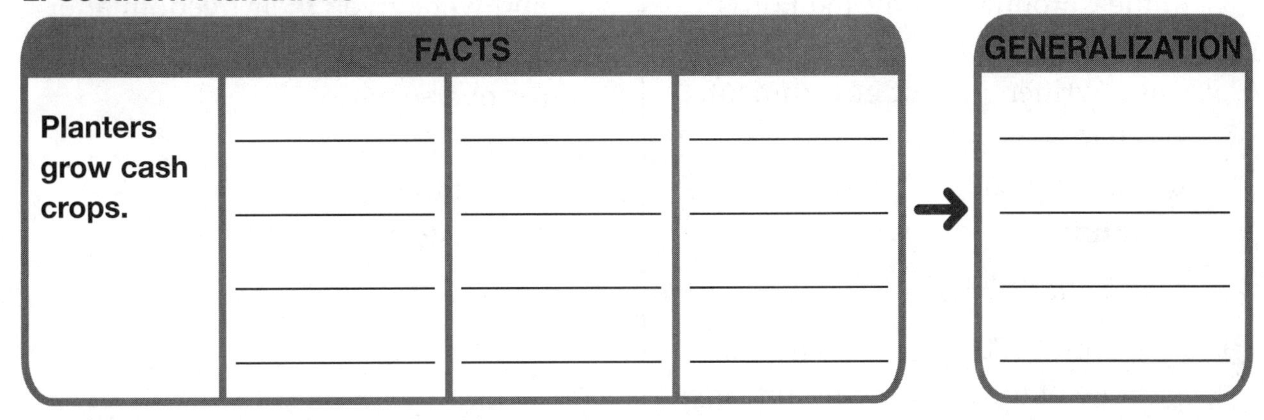

3. Southern Cities

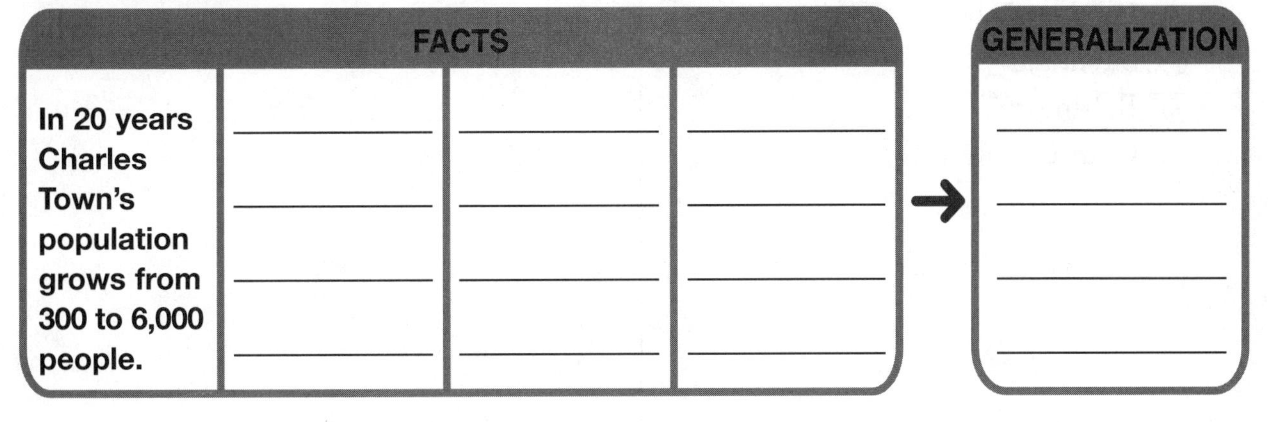

• CHAPTER •

7

Name ______________________ Date ____________

Test Preparation

Directions **Read each question and choose the best answer. Then fill in the circle for the answer you have chosen. Be sure to fill in the circle completely.**

1. The Calverts wanted to build a colony in North America to make money and provide a refuge for ______.
   - Ⓐ Puritans
   - Ⓑ Catholics
   - Ⓒ colonists
   - Ⓓ debtors

2. In the Carolina Colony, the Lords Proprietors wrote a ______, which was a written plan of government.
   - Ⓕ charter
   - Ⓖ action plan
   - Ⓗ ratification
   - Ⓙ constitution

3. By the mid-1700s ______, Virginia was one of the most important cities in the 13 colonies.
   - Ⓐ Williamsburg
   - Ⓑ Savannah
   - Ⓒ Baltimore
   - Ⓓ Charles Town

4. ______ owners became important leaders in the 13 colonies.
   - Ⓕ Ship
   - Ⓖ Sawmill
   - Ⓗ Plantation
   - Ⓙ Land

5. Unlike ______, indentured servants were not taken against their will and were given their freedom after a certain length of time.
   - Ⓐ overseers
   - Ⓑ slaves
   - Ⓒ debtors
   - Ⓓ masters

Use after reading Chapter 7, pages 230–253.

Name ______________________________ Date ______________

The French and Indian War Begins

Directions **Read the passage below and complete the activities that follow.**

General Braddock's Defeat

General Edward Braddock was appointed the commander of all British forces in the French and Indian War. His first goal was to capture Fort Duquesne, the French stronghold. In April 1755 he led more than 1,800 British and colonial troops westward across the mountains. The trip was long and difficult for the soldiers as they moved the large wagons and artillery across the rough trails.

Meanwhile, the French had learned of the British advance and were waiting. About 8 miles from Fort Duquesne, the French and their Native American allies attacked the British from behind trees and boulders. The British were trained to fight in open fields and had never fought an enemy this way. After the battle, almost two-thirds of the British troops were dead or wounded, including General Braddock. He died four days later.

Directions **For numbers 1–5, write *T* next to the statements that are true and *F* next to the statements that are false.**

1. ______ General Braddock was the commander of all British forces in the Revolutionary War.
2. ______ Braddock's army had a difficult journey to Fort Duquesne.
3. ______ The French were aware that Braddock's army was approaching.
4. ______ The British were trained to fight in wooded areas.
5. ______ General Braddock died immediately after being wounded on the battlefield.

Directions **For numbers 6–10, write *F* if the statement is a fact or *O* if the statement is an opinion.**

6. ______ The French were excellent fighters.
7. ______ The Native Americans were allies of the French.
8. ______ General Braddock was nervous about the journey to Fort Duquesne.
9. ______ Moving large artillery was difficult.
10. ______ Braddock's army consisted of British and colonial troops.

Name ______________________________ Date ______________

Britain Wins North America

Directions **Number the sentences below in the order in which each event occurred.**

_____ To make up for Spain's losses in the war, France gave Spain most of Louisiana and part of what is now Florida.

_____ Native Americans did not welcome the British colonists who wanted to settle in the Ohio Valley after the Treaty of Paris was signed.

_____ The British captured three forts: Fort Duquesne, Louisbourg, and Frontenac.

_____ The French and Indian War ended with the Treaty of Paris, giving Britain control of lands in present-day Canada and the area between the Appalachian Mountains and the Mississippi River.

_____ Many Native American fighters signed peace treaties with the British.

_____ French forces were defeated by General James Wolfe's British troops on the Plains of Abraham, near Quebec.

_____ The French gave up after the British captured Montreal.

_____ The British captured forts at Crown Point, Niagara, and Ticonderoga.

_____ Chief Pontiac united with other Native American tribes and attacked British forts.

_____ King George III issues the Proclamation of 1763 which prevents British colonists from buying, hunting, or exploring land west of the Appalachian Mountains.

(continued)

Use after reading Chapter 8, Lesson 2, pages 273–277.

Name ______________________________ Date ______________

Directions **Write your answer to each question.**

1. Why did King George III order the Proclamation of 1763?

____

____

____

2. What effects did the proclamation have on the life of the British colonists?

____

____

____

3. How did the American colonists feel about the proclamation? Why did they feel this way? ____

____

____

4. According to the British colonists, how did the Proclamation of 1763 conflict with the English Bill of Rights? ____

____

____

5. Did the proclamation stop colonists from settling west of the Appalachians? Explain. ____

____

____

Name ______________________ Date ______________

MAP AND GLOBE SKILLS

Compare Historical Maps

Directions **Use the maps to answer the questions on both pages.**

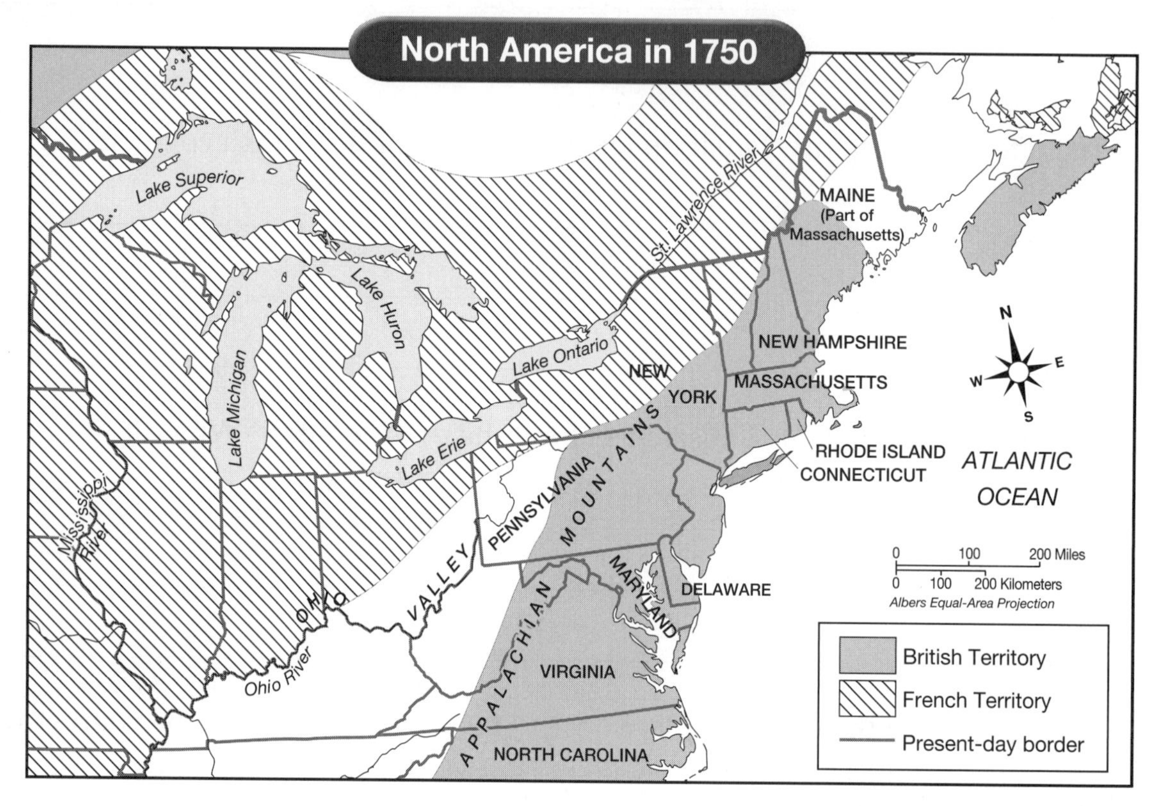

1. What pattern is used to show land originally claimed by the British and then given to the Native Americans? ______________________

2. According to the map, was any land claimed by the French in North America in 1763? ______________________

3. What land areas once claimed by the French were later claimed by the British?

____

4. Before the French and Indian War, who occupied the territory along the St. Lawrence River? ______________________

5. Before 1763 who claimed most of the land north of the Ohio River?

____

(continued)

Use after reading Chapter 8, Skill Lesson, pages 278–279.

Name ____________________ Date ____________

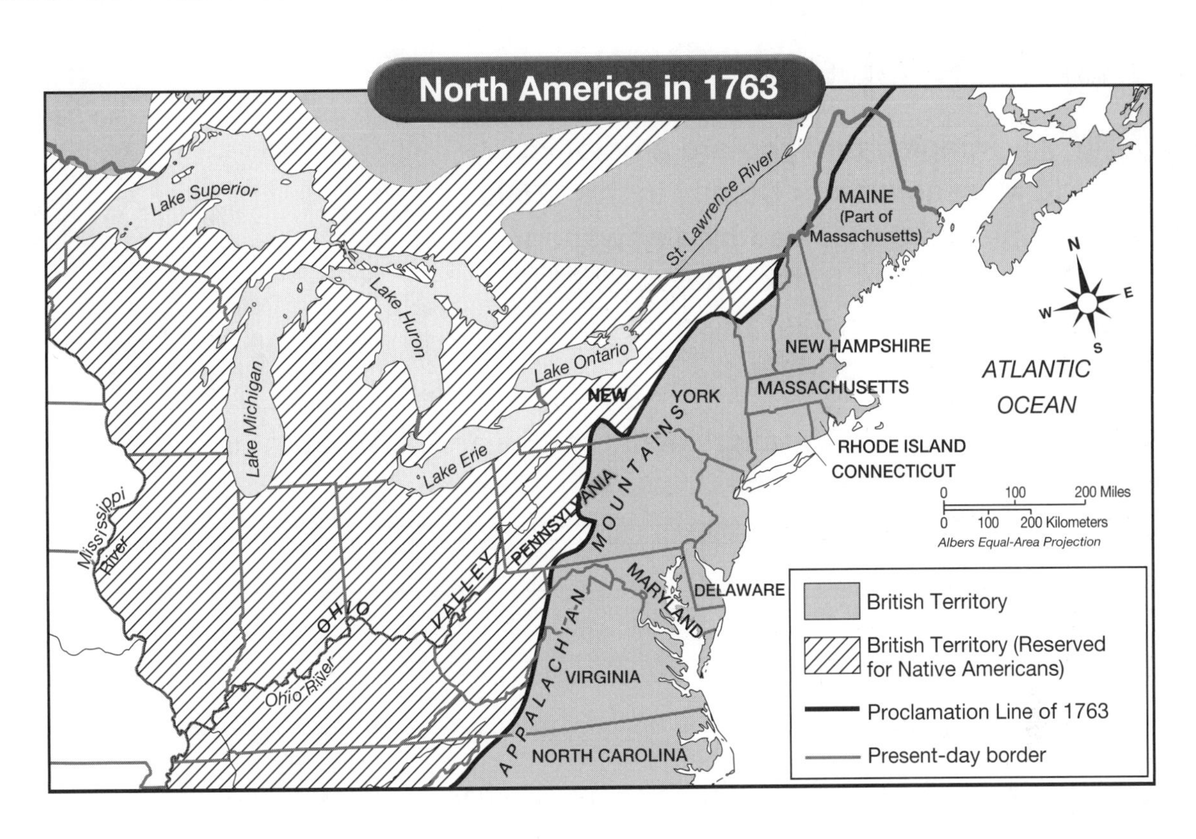

6. Who claimed the region of present-day Kentucky after the French and Indian War? ____________________

7. When did the British claim the regions bordering the Atlantic Ocean, such as Massachusetts, Connecticut, and Rhode Island? ____________________

____

8. Imagine that you are an explorer living in 1750. Write a description of the following journey: You start in what is now Maine and travel to the New York Colony, then to the region now known as Michigan, and then to the Ohio Valley region. How did you travel? Who claimed the land in which you traveled? What direction did you take? What kind of people did you encounter?

____

____

____

____

____

Name ______________________ Date ______________

Colonists Speak Out

Directions **Imagine that you are a colonist living in the Massachusetts Colony in the 1760s and you are being interviewed by a newspaper reporter. Write answers to the interview questions. Be sure to answer the questions from a colonist's point of view.**

1. Many people like you are angry about the Sugar Act. What is the Sugar Act, and why has it angered you? ______________________

2. Soon after the Sugar Act, the Stamp Act was enacted. How is the Stamp Act similar to the Sugar Act? ______________________

3. What can you do to show you are against taxation without representation? ______________________

4. Why are there so many British soldiers in Massachusetts and the other colonies? How do you feel about the soldiers being here? ______________________

Use after reading Chapter 8, Lesson 3, pages 280–285.

Name ______________________________ Date ______________

CITIZENSHIP SKILLS

Determine Point of View

Directions **Read each statement and then decide whose point of view the statement represents. Write either "Colonist" or "British leader" in the blank space before the sentence. In the second blank space explain why each person might hold this point of view.**

1. ______________________ We need money to help pay the cost of the French and Indian War.

____

____

2. ______________________ The Sugar Act is unjust. We had no representation when this law was decided.

____

____

3. ______________________ Patrick Henry has committed treason. He is working against his government.

____

____

4. ______________________ We need to work together instead of acting separately. We should talk with other colonial leaders to discuss what to do about the Stamp Act.

____

____

____

5. ______________________ We do not want "lobsters" and "redcoats" in our cities!

____

____

Name ______________________ Date ______________

The Road to War

Directions **Use the Word Bank to complete each sentence.**

Lexington	quarter
Samuel Adams	monopoly
Minutemen	Sons of Liberty
petition	Paul Revere
Intolerable Acts	blockade

1. Parliament wanted to give the East India Company a ______________________ on tea.

2. ______________________ believed in the use of violence only when all else failed.

3. A group of men called the ______________________ boarded ships and dumped tea into the harbor.

4. To keep ships from entering or leaving Boston Harbor, Parliament ordered a ______________________.

5. Colonists were punished by having to ______________________ British soldiers.

6. The colonists called Parliament's new laws the ______________________.

7. The First Continental Congress sent Parliament a ______________________, which stated that colonists had a right to "life, liberty, and property."

8. Colonists in Massachusetts organized a militia made up of ______________________.

9. When he learned the British were coming, ______________________ rode to Lexington to warn fellow colonists.

10. The fighting at ______________________ and Concord marked the beginning of the Revolutionary War.

Use after reading Chapter 8, Lesson 4, pages 288–292.

Name ______________________ Date ______________

The Second Continental Congress

Directions **Imagine that you are a member of the Second Continental Congress. Write a letter to King George III explaining why you believe the colonies in North America should be allowed to peacefully separate from Britain.**

Think about these questions as you write your letter:

What was John Dickinson's point of view on war?

How many people died in the battle at Breed's Hill?

How might a petition help?

Who, other than the British and colonists, might be affected by war?

Name ______________________ Date ____________

Events Unite the Colonies

Directions **Complete this graphic organizer to show that you understand the causes and effects of some of the key events that helped unite the colonies.**

Cause	→	Effect
The British Parliament needs extra money to pay for the French and Indian War.	→	____________________ ____________________
____________________ ____________________	→	The Boston Tea Party takes place in Boston Harbor in December 1773.
The British Parliament passes the Intolerable Acts to punish the colonists.	→	____________________ ____________________
____________________ ____________________	→	The Second Continental Congress is held in Philadelphia in May 1775.
The Battle of Bunker Hill takes place near Boston on June 17, 1775.	→	____________________ ____________________

Use after reading Chapter 8, pages 267–297.

• CHAPTER •
8

Name ________________________ Date ______________

Test Preparation

Directions **Read each question and choose the best answer. Then fill in the circle for the answer you have chosen. Be sure to fill in the circle completely.**

1. The French and Indian War began because both France and Britain believed they owned the area known as—
   - Ⓐ Pennsylvania.
   - Ⓑ the Appalachians.
   - Ⓒ the Ohio Valley.
   - Ⓓ New France.

2. Chief Pontiac's rebellion began because he—
   - Ⓕ believed he owned the Ohio Valley region.
   - Ⓖ wanted to stop the loss of Indian hunting lands.
   - Ⓗ had formed an alliance with France.
   - Ⓙ wanted to rule British forts.

3. Why were colonists angered by the tax laws passed by the British Parliament?
   - Ⓐ They believed they should have a voice in deciding such laws.
   - Ⓑ They were too poor to pay the taxes.
   - Ⓒ They thought the taxes were unfair.
   - Ⓓ They believed they shouldn't have to pay any taxes.

4. Which of the following was an Intolerable Act?
   - Ⓕ preventing the Massachusetts legislature from making laws
   - Ⓖ banning any town meetings not authorized by the governor
   - Ⓗ forcing colonists to quarter British soldiers
   - Ⓙ all of the above

5. The first united colonial army was called—
   - Ⓐ the Continental Army.
   - Ⓑ the Hessian Army.
   - Ⓒ the Mercenary Army.
   - Ⓓ the Loyalist Army.

Name ______________________________ Date ______________

Independence Is Declared

Directions **Use words and phrases from the Word Bank to complete each sentence below.**

public opinion	Preamble	resolution
allegiance	independence	grievances

1. The point of view held by most people is called ______________________.
2. The colonists wanted ______________________, the freedom to govern themselves.
3. Another word for loyalty is ______________________.
4. Richard Henry Lee wrote a formal statement, known as a ______________________, describing the feelings of the colonists.
5. The first part of the Declaration of Independence is called the ______________________.
6. The complaints, or ______________________, against the British king and Parliament were part of the Declaration of Independence.

(continued)

Name ______________________________ Date ______________

Directions **Match each person with the correct description. Write the letter of the correct person on the blank provided. Some letters may be used more than once.**

	Description	Name
7	______ first to sign the Declaration of Independence	**A.** John Dickinson
8	______ wrote the Declaration of Independence	**B.** John Adams
9	______ wrote a letter to his wife Abigail describing the first public reading of the Declaration of Independence	**C.** John Nixon
10	______ published *Common Sense* in January, 1776	**D.** John Hancock
11	______ helped write the Articles of the Confederation	**E.** Thomas Paine
12	______ read the Declaration of Independence to the Second Continental Congress	**F.** Thomas Jefferson
13	______ wrote *A Summary View of the Rights of British America*	
14	______ called for a revolution before the Declaration of Independence was written	

Name ____________________ Date ____________

Americans and the Revolution

Directions **Read the passage below. When you have finished, write a paragraph trying to persuade someone to choose a different position in the Revolutionary War. For example, you may try to persuade a Loyalist to become a Patriot.**

As the Revolutionary War began, most colonists held one of four opinions. Those who supported the British king and Parliament were called **Loyalists.** They wanted to work out the differences between the colonies and Britain. Those people who were **Patriots** wanted to break from Britain and form a new country. They believed they could establish a better government if they were independent.

Some people wanted to wait and see what would happen. They did not want to take either side. They were **neutral** about the matter of independence and willing to accept whatever happened. Some people, such as Quakers, were opposed to war for any reason. They were known as **pacifists,** or people who believe in settling disagreements peacefully.

 Use after reading Chapter 9, Lesson 2, pages 308–312.

Name ______________________________ Date ______________

CITIZENSHIP SKILLS

Make a Decision

Directions **The Revolutionary War has begun. How will you respond? Explain your decision, based on the questions below.**

Steps in Making a Decision

1. Know that you have to make a decision.

   You have the choice of fighting for the British or for the colonists.

2. Gather information.

   What do you need to know before deciding? Where might you find the information you need?

   ____

   ____

3. Identify your choices.

   There are at least two choices, as given above. Are there other choices you could make?

   ____

   ____

4. Predict consequences, and weigh those consequences.

   List each of the choices with its consequences. If a consequence seems very important to you, put a star next to it.

   ____

   ____

5. Make a choice, and take action.

   What will you decide?

   ____

   ____

Name ______________________________ Date ______________

Fighting the Revolutionary War

Directions **Follow the instructions below. Write your answers on the map.**

1. Draw a star next to the battle known as the turning point of the war.
2. Circle the place where Ethan Allen and the Green Mountain boys were victorious.
3. Draw a snowflake next to the place where Washington's troops spent the winter of 1777.
4. Draw a pitcher at the battle where Mary Ludwig Hays McCauley brought water to the soldiers.
5. Draw a boat where Washington surprised Hessian mercenaries on Christmas Day, 1776.

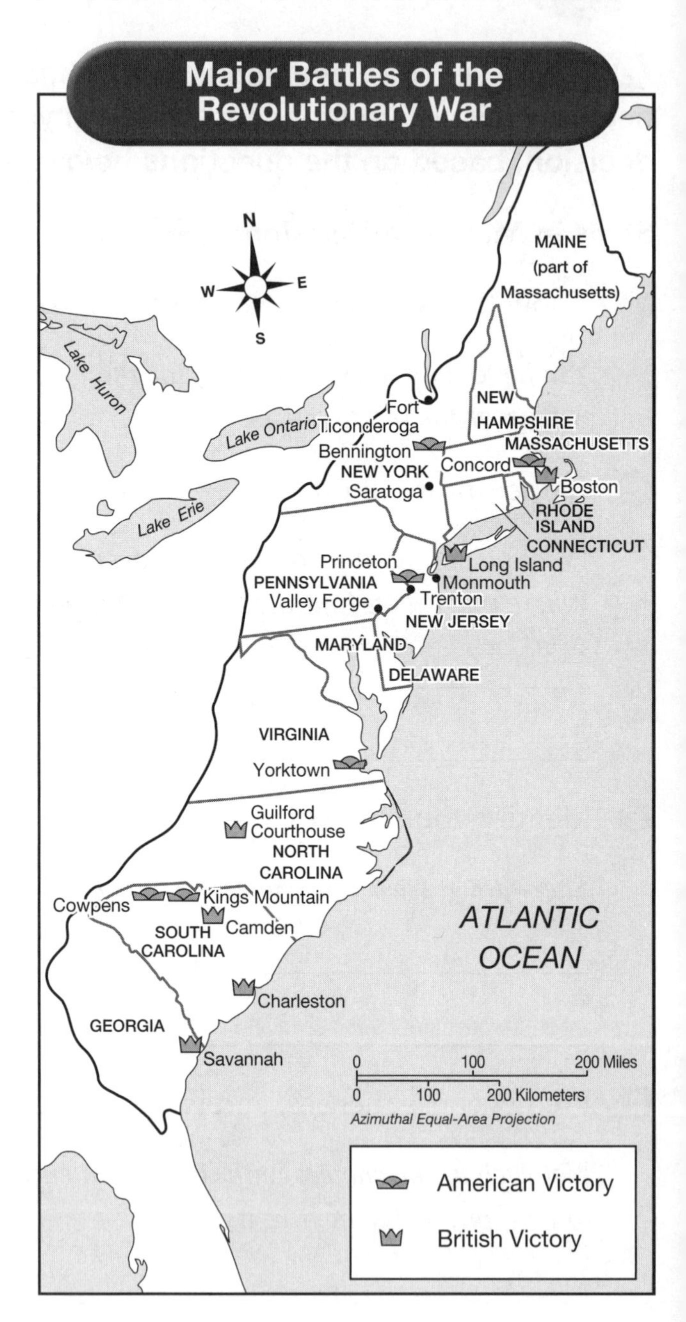

Use after reading Chapter 9, Lesson 3, pages 314–319.

Name ______________________ Date ______________

Independence Is Won

Directions **Complete the time line using the choices listed below. Write the number of the event next to the correct marker on the time line.**

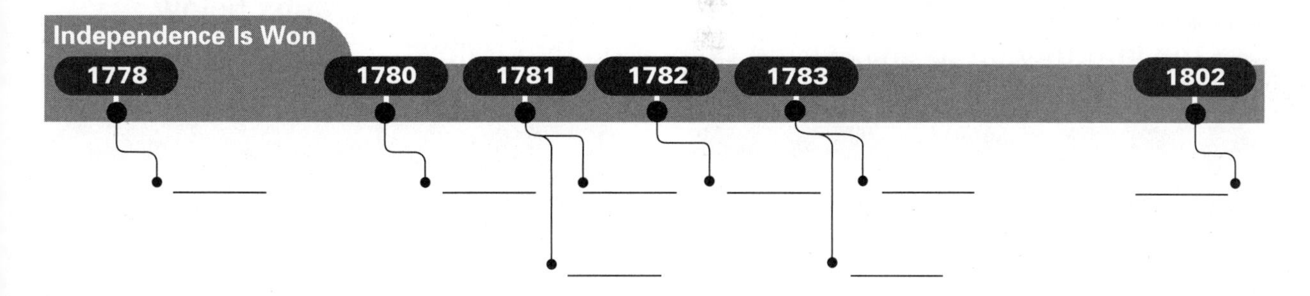

1. British capture Charleston, South Carolina
2. George Washington returns to Virginia
3. British capture Savannah, Georgia
4. Britain and the United States sign the Treaty of Paris
5. The United States Military Academy is founded at West Point
6. British surrender at Yorktown
7. Britian and the United States send representatives to Paris
8. The Continental Army wins the Battle of Cowpens

Name ______________________ Date ____________

CHART AND GRAPH SKILLS

Compare Graphs

Directions **Look at the information presented in the bar graphs below. Use the information to answer the questions that follow.**

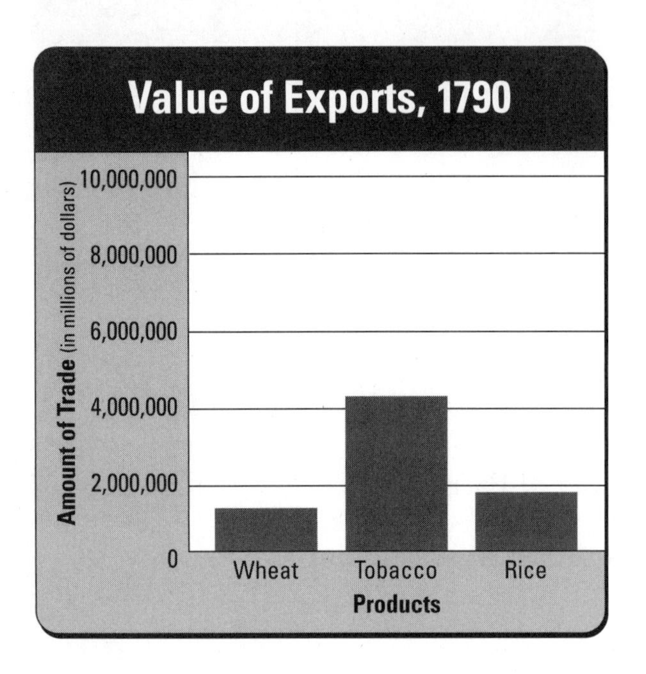

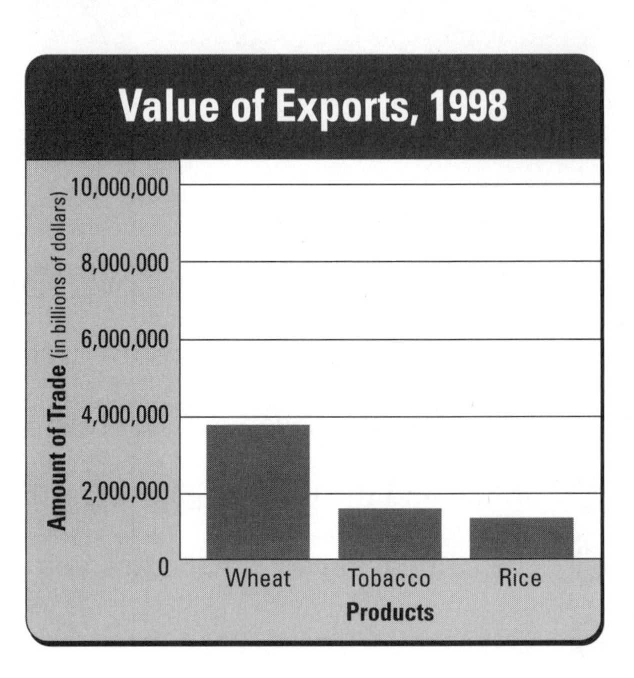

1. Compare the two graphs. How has the relative importance of each item's dollar value changed? ______________________

   ____

   ____

   ____

2. About how much more valuable were tobacco exports compared to wheat exports in 1790? ______________________

3. About how much more valuable were wheat exports compared to tobacco exports in 1998? ______________________

   ____

(continued)

Use after reading Chapter 9, Skill Lesson, pages 330–331.

Name ______________________ Date ______________

Directions **Look at the information presented in the line graphs below. Use the graphs to answer the questions that follow.**

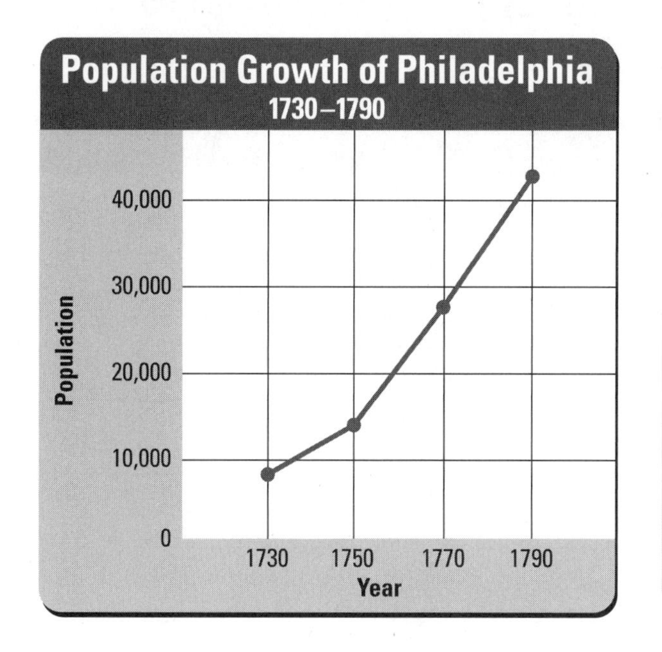

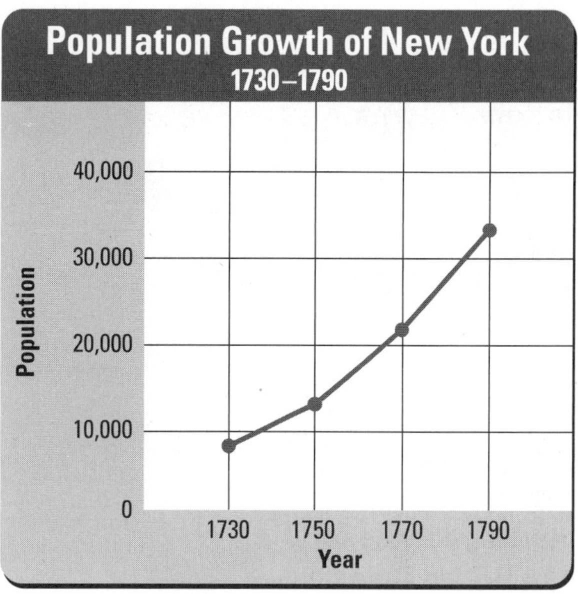

4. Which city grew faster from 1730 to 1790? ______________________

5. In what years were the two cities equal or nearly equal in population?

____

6. In 1770 how many more people lived in Philadelphia than in New York?

____

7. By how many times did the population of Philadelphia grow over the 60 years the graph covers? ______________________

8. What was the growth in New York during the same time period?

____

Name ______________________ Date ____________

Independence is Declared

Directions **Complete this graphic organizer by putting the events in the correct sequence.**

FIRST		NEXT		LAST
Colonists in North America want independence for the 13 British Colonies	→	______________________	→	______________________

Use after reading Chapter 9, pages 301–331.

· CHAPTER ·

9

Name ______________________ Date ______________

Test Preparation

Directions **Read each question and choose the best answer. Then fill in the circle for the answer you have chosen. Be sure to fill in the circle completely.**

1. Which of the following was **not** a reason American colonists wanted to break with Britain in 1776?
   - Ⓐ taxes
   - Ⓑ no representation
   - Ⓒ religious freedom
   - Ⓓ war had already begun

2. Who was the author of the Declaration of Independence?
   - Ⓕ Thomas Paine
   - Ⓖ John Adams
   - Ⓗ Richard Henry Lee
   - Ⓙ Thomas Jefferson

3. People who remained neutral in the war—
   - Ⓐ sided with the colonists.
   - Ⓑ took neither side.
   - Ⓒ did not believe war was right.
   - Ⓓ were loyal to Britain.

4. Which of the following countries did **not** send help to the colonies?
   - Ⓕ Scotland
   - Ⓖ France
   - Ⓗ Poland
   - Ⓙ Spain

5. General Cornwallis surrendered at the Battle of—
   - Ⓐ Fort Ticonderoga.
   - Ⓑ Saratoga.
   - Ⓒ Charlestown.
   - Ⓓ Yorktown.

Name ______________________ Date ______________

The Confederation Period

Directions **Each statement below is false. For each sentence, cross out the wrong word. Then, in the blank at the end of the sentence, write the word that would make the sentence true.**

1. After the war with Britain ended, Congress printed too much money, causing terrible rebellion. ______________________

2. A form of government in which people elect representatives to govern the country is called a dictatorship. ______________________

3. Decision making required representation from at least five states.

   ____

4. Shays's Rebellion started over army policy. ______________________

5. Shays's Rebellion took place in Virginia. ______________________

6. An arsenal is a place to store food. ______________________

7. A territory is land that belongs to the state government but is not represented in Congress. ______________________

8. Congress passed an arsenal, or set of laws, to measure the western lands.

   ____

9. The newly settled lands were called the Southeast Territory.

   ____

10. Townships were 8 miles on each side. ______________________

11. The new lands were to offer private schools to everyone.

    ____

Use after reading Chapter 10, Lesson 1, pages 346–350.

Name ______________________________ Date ______________

The Constitutional Convention

Directions **Read the following list of issues debated at the Constitutional Convention. Match the resolution of each one with the correct issue. Write the letter of the correct resolution on the blank provided.**

1. ______ the relationship between the states and national government
2. ______ representation of each state in Congress
3. ______ the issue of enslaved African Americans

A. the Three-Fifths Compromise

B. a federal system of shared powers

C. a system of two houses of Congress

Directions **Read each sentence below, and fill in the blank with the correct term. Use the words from the Word Bank.**

George Read	George Washington	Roger Sherman
Rhode Island	Benjamin Franklin	

4. All the states except ______________________ sent delegates to Philadelphia.
5. The oldest member of the convention was ______________________.
6. The delegates elected ______________________ president of the convention.
7. ______________________ believed that states should be done away with altogether.
8. The Connecticut Compromise was created by ______________________.

Name ______________________ Date ____________

The Three Branches of Government

Directions **Read the list below of positions in the government. In the space provided, name the correct branch of government for each one. Then write a brief description of the qualifications and duties of the person holding that job.**

1. President ______________________

____

____

____

____

____

____

____

2. Supreme Court Justice ______________________

____

____

____

____

____

3. Representative ______________________

____

____

____

____

____

Use after reading Chapter 10, Lesson 3, pages 358–363.

Name ______________________ Date ______________

CHART AND GRAPH SKILLS

Read a Flow Chart

Directions **Fill in the flow chart to show the jobs in each of the three branches of government. In the second row, describe the main task of each branch. Some examples have been filled in for you.**

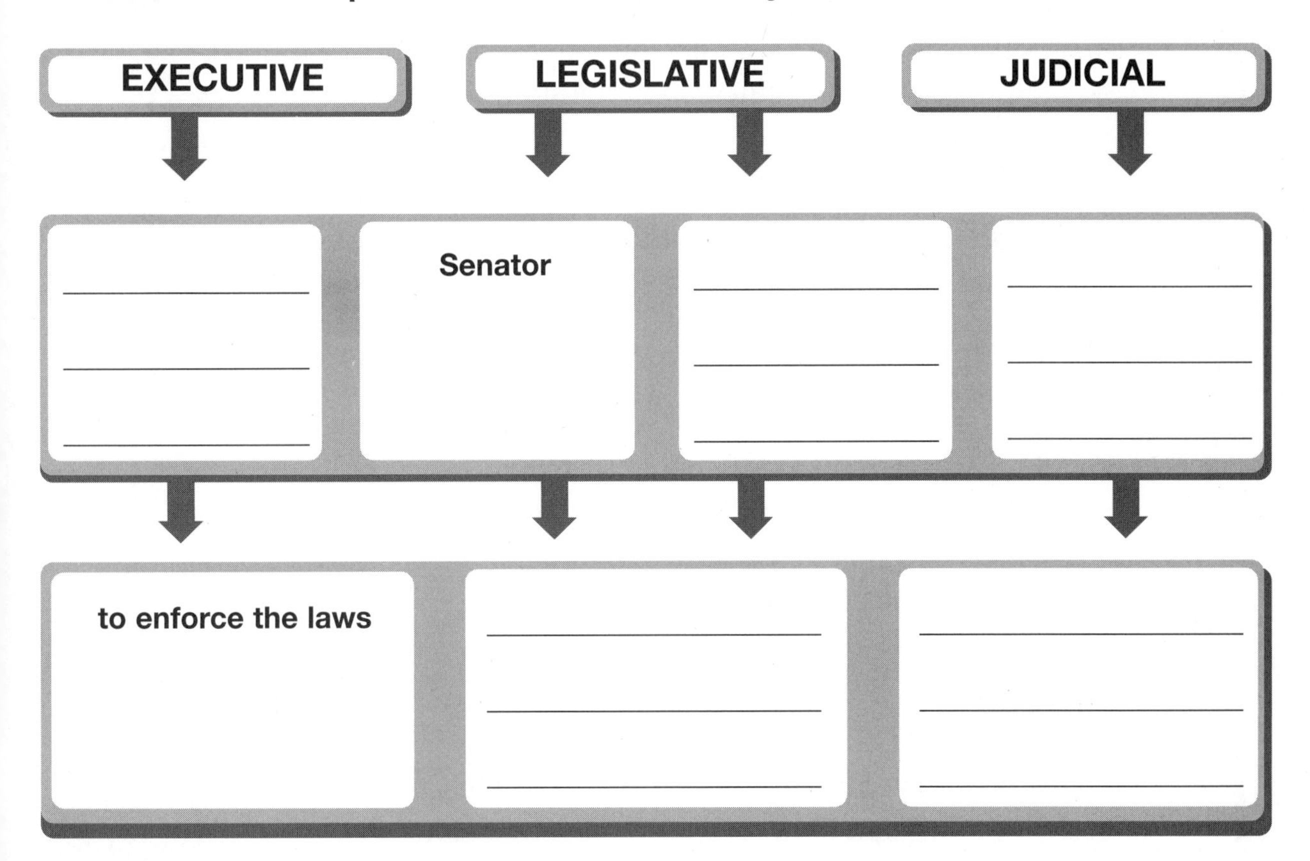

Name ______________________________ Date ______________

Approval and the Bill of Rights

Directions **Read the freedoms guaranteed by the Bill of Rights. Then read each statement that follows. If the statement is a fact, write *F* in the blank. If the statement is an opinion, write *O* in the blank.**

1. People may follow any religion. The government cannot financially support or promote any religion. People have freedom to speak, to publish, and to hold meetings.

2. People may keep and bear weapons.

3. People do not have to board soldiers in their homes during peacetimes.

4. The government cannot search people's homes or remove their property without the permission of a judge.

5–8. People have the right to a fair trial by a jury. Defendants do not have to testify against themselves. They may have a lawyer represent them in court. They cannot be tried twice for the same crime.

9. People have other rights not specifically listed in the Constitution.

10. The federal government can do only what the Constitution gives it permission to do. All other powers belong to the states and to the people.

1. ______ It is not fair to have soldiers sleeping in your home at any time.
2. ______ People can hold public meetings to talk about their government.
3. ______ Newspapers should print only good news.
4. ______ The federal government has gotten too powerful.
5. ______ A person cannot be tried twice for the same crime.
6. ______ The individual states do not have enough power.
7. ______ People do not have to testify against themselves in court.

 Use after reading Chapter 10, Lesson 4, pages 366–372.

Name ______________________________ Date ______________

CITIZENSHIP SKILLS

Act as a Responsible Citizen

Directions **Citizens have responsibilities as well as rights and privileges. Read each statement below the picture. Then suggest how a responsible citizen might handle the situation.**

1. You notice that people are being careless about litter in your neighborhood.

____

____

2. Several dogs in your neighborhood are not on leashes.

____

3. Skateboarders in your neighborhood are practicing on sidewalks and in the street.

____

____

4. A local election is coming up. ______________________________

____

5. A new law is coming up for discussion before being voted on. Some people disagree with the law. ______________________________

____

____

Name ______________________ Date __________

The New Government Begins

Directions The two major political parties of the late eighteenth century differed in several ways. Fill out the chart below to show how they were different. One example has been given.

FEDERALIST	REPUBLICAN
Believed in a strong central government	Believed that the powers of the national government should be limited to those stated in the Constitution

Use after reading Chapter 10, Lesson 5, pages 374–379.

Name ______________________________ Date ______________

A New Form of Government

Directions **Complete this graphic organizer by summarizing the facts about the writing and ratification of the United States Constitution.**

TOPIC OR EVENT

The Constitutional Convention

→

IMPORTANT DETAILS

What?

____

____

Who?
Delegates from 12 of the 13 United States

Where?

____

How?

____

Why?

____

____

____

____

____

____

____

→

SUMMARY

____

____

____

____

____

____

____

____

____

____

____

____

____

____

____

____

Name ______________________ Date ______________

Test Preparation

Directions **Read each question and choose the best answer. Then fill in the circle for the answer you have chosen. Be sure to fill in the circle completely.**

1. ______ was one good reason for changing the weak national government set up by the Articles of Confederation.
   - Ⓐ The Northwest Ordinance
   - Ⓑ The way Congress moved around
   - Ⓒ Shays's Rebellion
   - Ⓓ The idea of James Madison

2. The Great Compromise established—
   - Ⓕ how enslaved African Americans would be counted.
   - Ⓖ who had the right to tax.
   - Ⓗ the balance between state and federal government.
   - Ⓙ how states would be represented in Congress.

3. A President who does not perform the duties of the office can be—
   - Ⓐ impeached by Congress.
   - Ⓑ forced to leave town.
   - Ⓒ tried before the Supreme Court.
   - Ⓓ sent to a foreign country.

4. The Bill of Rights was influenced by the—
   - Ⓕ Spanish constitution.
   - Ⓖ British Magna Carta.
   - Ⓗ Italian Bill of Rights.
   - Ⓙ French political practice.

5. George Washington set an example for future Presidents by—
   - Ⓐ riding a white horse.
   - Ⓑ placing his friends in government positions.
   - Ⓒ serving only two elected terms.
   - Ⓓ naming the person to be the next President.

Use after reading Chapter 10, pages 344–379.

Name ______________________ Date ______________

The Louisiana Purchase

Directions **Read each numbered item below. Fill in each blank with the name of the person or persons connected to the description. Use names from the Word Bank. You may use a name more than once.**

Sacagawea	Thomas Jefferson	Meriwether Lewis	Zebulon Pike
York	William Clark	Napoleon Bonaparte	

1. hoped to revive French power in North America

   ____

2. wanted the United States to have a port on the lower Mississippi River

   ____

3. needed money to fight a war ______________________________

4. leaders of the Corps of Discovery ______________________________

   ____

5. African American who helped the Corps of Discovery by hunting and fishing

   ____

6. helped the Corps of Discovery by guiding them through the land of the Shoshones ______________________________

7. explored the southwestern portion of the Louisiana Purchase

   ____

Name ______________________ Date ____________

The War of 1812

Directions **Look at the time line below. Match the events with the correct date on the time line. Place the letter of the correct event in the blank provided.**

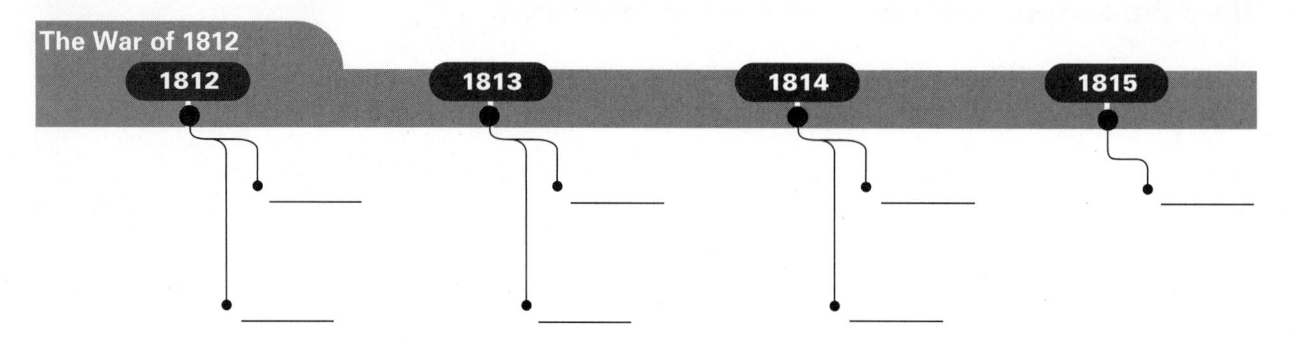

A. Battle of Lake Erie

B. United States declares war against Britain

C. Battle of New Orleans

D. British burn Washington, D.C.

E. Francis Scott Key writes "The Defense of Fort McHenry"

F. The warship *Constitution* defeats the British ship *Guerriére*.

G. Battle of the Thames

(continued)

Use after reading Chapter 11, Lesson 2, pages 389–394.

Name ____________________ Date ____________

Directions **Answer the questions below.**

1. Give two reasons that the United States declared war on Britain.

____

____

____

____

2. What United States senator believed that the United States should "take the whole continent"? _______________

3. What was the nickname of the warship *Constitution*? _______________

4. What Shawnee Indian leader was killed at the Battle of the Thames?

____

5. What action did Dolley Madison take before leaving the White House?

____

____

6. What did Francis Scott Key do after seeing the battle at Fort McHenry?

____

____

7. What years came to be known as the Era of Good Feelings?

____

8. Why was the Battle of New Orleans unnecessary? _______________

____

____

____

Name ______________________ Date ____________

The Age of Jackson

Directions Read the paragraph below. Fill in the graphic organizer to show why the United States Supreme Court said the Cherokees could keep their land. Then answer the questions that follow.

United States Supreme Court Chief Justice John Marshall wrote the opinion of the Court in the case of *Worcester* v. *Georgia*. Marshall referred to Britain's past treaties with the Cherokee. He said the Cherokee had honored the treaties. That proved that the Cherokee were a nation able to govern themselves. He also argued that the laws of Georgia had no power over the Cherokee nation people because they were a "distinct community." Finally, Marshall said that the Native Americans had previous possession of the land. It was theirs. Unfortunately, President Andrew Jackson refused to accept the ruling. He said, "John Marshall has made his decision; now let him enforce it." Jackson then ordered federal troops to remove the Native Americans and take the land.

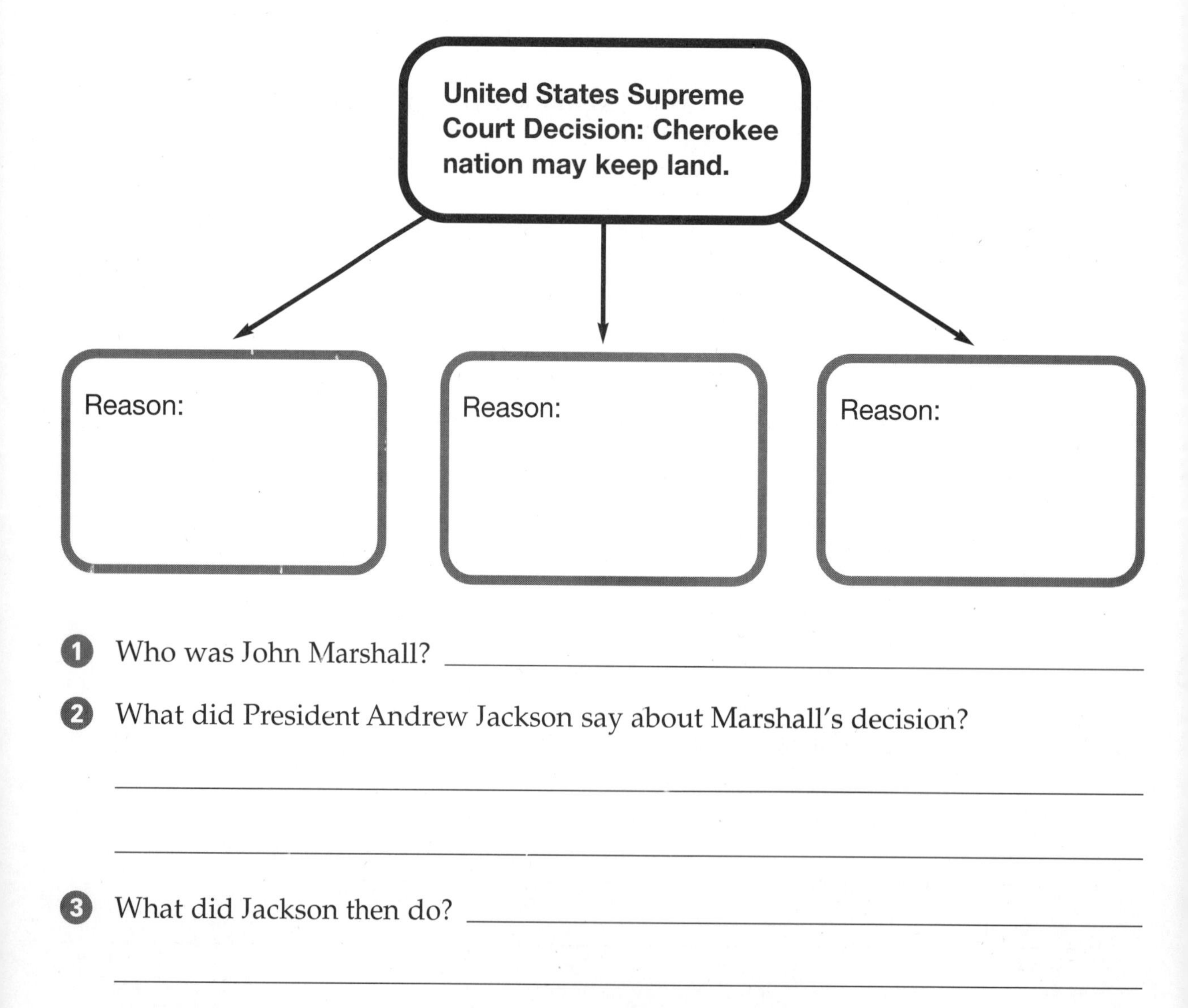

1. Who was John Marshall? ______________________

2. What did President Andrew Jackson say about Marshall's decision?

____

____

3. What did Jackson then do? ______________________

____

Use after reading Chapter 11, Lesson 3, pages 395–399.

Name ______________________ Date ______________

From Ocean to Ocean

Directions **Fill in the blanks in the paragraph below, using terms from the Word Bank.**

Mormons	gold rush	dictator	forty-niners
Oregon	Cession	manifest destiny	

In the early 1800s many people began to believe that the United States should stretch from the Atlantic Ocean to the Pacific Ocean. This idea was known as ______________________. In time, this goal seemed possible. In 1834 when General Santa Anna took over the Mexican government and made himself ______________________, Texas settlers were alarmed. After battles at the Alamo and San Jacinto, the settlers defeated Santa Anna and Texas became an independent republic. Several years later, Mexico and the United States again clashed over the Texas border. Mexico agreed to give up its claims in what was called the Mexican ______________________. In addition, some people went west in search of religious freedom. The ______________________ settled in Utah after being driven from Illinois. Marcus and Narcissa Whitman went to the ______________________ Territory to set up missions. Finally, when gold was discovered in California, a ______________________ began. Those who went called themselves ______________________ because many settlers moved there in 1849.

Use after reading Chapter 11, Lesson 4, pages 402–409.

Name ______________________ Date ______________

MAP AND GLOBE SKILLS

Identifying Changing Borders

Directions Use the map below to answer the questions that follow.

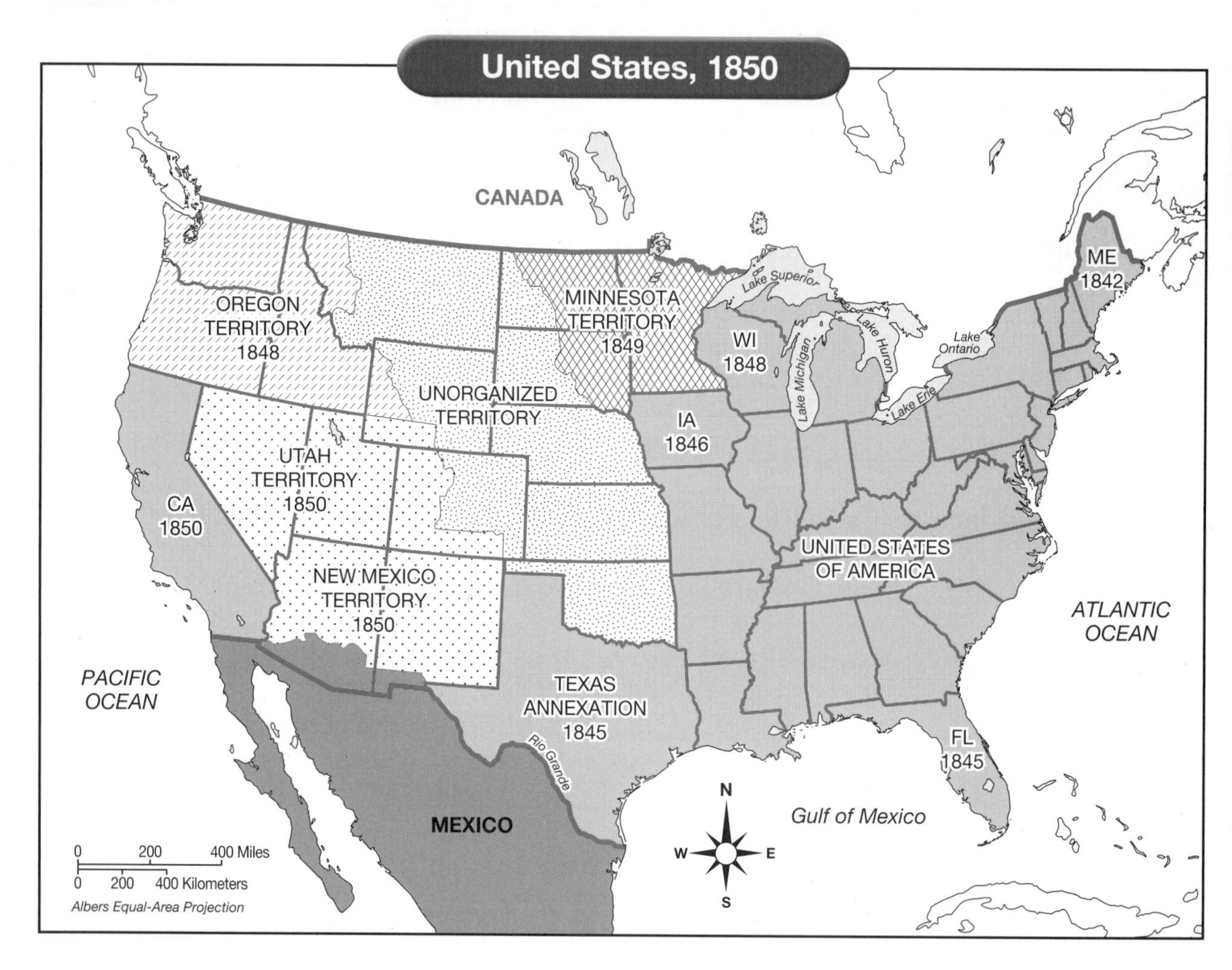

1. In what year did the United States gain control of the Utah Territory? __________

2. What state was the farthest west in 1850? __________

3. What river eventually became the border between Mexico and the United States?

____

4. By 1850 had the idea of manifest destiny been achieved? Explain.

____

____

____

Use after reading Chapter 11, Skill Lesson, pages 410–411.

Name ______________________________ Date ______________

An Industrial Revolution

Directions **Tell how each invention listed below played a part in the Industrial Revolution. Write your answers on the blanks provided.**

1. The steam engine ______________________________

____

2. Cotton mills ______________________________

____

____

3. Interchangeable parts ______________________________

____

4. Cotton gin ______________________________

____

5. Mechanical reaper ______________________________

____

Name ______________________ Date ____________

America and the Industrial Revolution

Directions **Complete this graphic organizer by drawing conclusions about the Industrial Revolution.**

WHAT YOU KNOW		NEW FACTS		CONCLUSION
	→	Life was often difficult for Americans, especially those who chose to settle in unexplored lands.	↘	
	→	With new inventions like the reaper, wheat that once took two weeks to cut could now be cut in one day.	→	
	→	By the mid-1800s more than 88 thousand miles of road and 9 thousand miles of rail had been built in the United States.	↗	

Use after reading Chapter 11, pages 383–419.

· CHAPTER ·

11

Name ______________________ Date ____________

Test Preparation

Directions **Read each question and choose the best answer. Then fill in the circle for the answer you have chosen. Be sure to fill in the circle completely.**

1. Napoleon was willing to sell Louisiana because—
   - Ⓐ he knew he was too far away to control it.
   - Ⓑ he had no use for the land.
   - Ⓒ he needed money to fight a war.
   - Ⓓ he was persuaded by Jefferson's representatives.

2. The years from 1817 to 1825 are called—
   - Ⓕ the Age of Jackson.
   - Ⓖ manifest destiny.
   - Ⓗ the Monroe Doctrine.
   - Ⓙ the Era of Good Feelings.

3. All of the following are reasons for Andrew Jackson's election *except* that—
   - Ⓐ he was a war hero.
   - Ⓑ he had lots of money.
   - Ⓒ for the first time all white men could vote.
   - Ⓓ he was considered a common man.

4. During the 1850s, settlers moving west followed the—
   - Ⓕ Erie Canal.
   - Ⓖ Oregon Trail.
   - Ⓗ Royal Road.
   - Ⓙ Northwest Passage.

5. *Tom Thumb* proved that—
   - Ⓐ steam-powered railroad engines were faster than horses.
   - Ⓑ locomotives were undependable.
   - Ⓒ steam-powered railroad cars had better pulling power than horses.
   - Ⓓ trains needed much improvement to be practical.

Name ______________________ Date ____________

Regional Disagreements

Directions **Read the passage below. Then fill in the chart that follows, showing the differences between the North and South.**

The North and the South could not come to an agreement about slavery. Northerners did not think that slavery should be allowed to spread to the western territories, while Southerners thought they had the right to take their enslaved workers west with them—just as they would take their other property.

The Northern economy relied on manufacturing and shipping, not agriculture, so the North did not need laborers as the South did. Also, many Northerners thought that slavery was wrong and should be abolished, or done away with. Those Northerners were called abolitionists, and they wanted all people to be free. Even Northerners who were not abolitionists did not want more slave states added to the country.

However, the economy of the South depended on laborers. Plantation owners were able to harvest more cotton, indigo, and tobacco by using slaves to work in the fields. Those Southerners believed that individual states had the right to decide whether people could have slaves.

	North	South
Economy based on		
Viewed slavery as		
Ideas about extending slavery		

Directions **Use the passage and chart above to answer the questions.**

1. What were Northerners called who did not agree with slavery? Why were they called that? ______________________

____

2. Where did most Northerners believe slavery should not be allowed to spread?

____

Use after reading Chapter 12, Lesson 1, pages 436–441.

Name ______________________________ Date ______________

CITIZENSHIP SKILLS

Identify Frame of Reference

Directions **Read the material below and then answer the questions.**

Henry Clay

When Missouri asked to be a state in 1819, Henry Clay was a congress member from Kentucky. Although Clay owned slaves, he did not want slavery to divide the country. He worked very hard to find a solution that would make both the North and the South happy. While other members of Congress were arguing for their region of the country, Clay said, "I know no South, no North, no East, no West, to which I owe any allegiance [loyalty]." His solution was called the Missouri Compromise.

John Quincy Adams

John Quincy Adams, a Northerner, was the secretary of state at the time. Adams kept a diary, and in February 1820 he wrote about what he thought the future might bring, ". . . if the dissolution [breaking apart] of the Union should result from the slave question, it is as obvious as anything. . . that it must shortly afterwards be followed by the universal emancipation [freeing] of the slaves. . ."

1. What viewpoint did Henry Clay have about the Union? How do you know?

____

____

____

2. What did John Quincy Adams think would happen if the Union broke apart?

____

Name ______________________________ Date ______________

Slavery and Freedom

Directions **On the blanks provided, write the word or name that best completes each sentence. Some letters in your answers will have numbers under them. Write these letters in the appropriate boxes below, and you will find the name of the most famous conductor of the Underground Railroad.**

1. A man named _ _ _   _ _ _ _ _ _ led the first slave rebellion.
   (7)

2. Something done in secret is done _ _ _ _ _ _ _ _ _ _ _.
   (3)

3. A person who is running away is a _ _ _ _ _ _ _ _.
   (9)

4. To act against slavery is to _ _ _ _ _ _ it.
   (4)

5. The Virginia legislature debated the _ _ _ _ _ _ _ _ _ _ _ _, or freeing, of slaves.
   (11) (2)

6. Sets of laws, known as slave _ _ _ _ _, ruled the lives of slaves.
   (6)

7. Harriet Beecher Stowe wrote a book titled _ _ _ _ _   _ _ _'_   _ _ _ _ _.
   (8) (13)

8. The newspaper *Freedom's Journal* called for _ _ _ _ _ _ _ _, or equal rights for all people.
   (12)

9. Someone who wants to end slavery is called an _ _ _ _ _ _ _ _ _ _ _ _.
   (10) (5)

10. A former slave named _ _ _ _ _ _ _ _ _   _ _ _ _ _ traveled the country to speak out against slavery.
    (1)

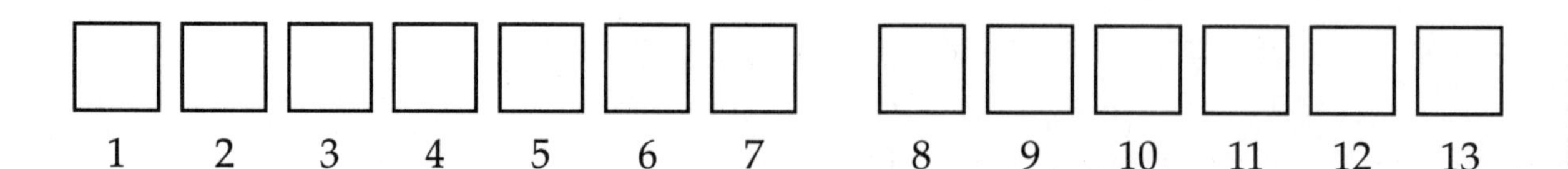

1 2 3 4 5 6 7   8 9 10 11 12 13

Use after reading Chapter 12, Lesson 2, pages 444–449.

Name ______________________________ Date ______________

The Union Breaks Apart

Directions **Read the passage below. Then read each statement that follows. If the statement is true, write *T* in the blank. If the statement is false, write *F* in the blank.**

Abraham Lincoln had barely a year of formal schooling, but he learned to read and write. He was very intelligent and read everything he could. Growing up, Lincoln had many jobs such as a rail-splitter, riverboat man, store clerk, and postmaster. After studying very hard on his own, he finally became a lawyer.

About five years later, in 1842, Abe Lincoln married Mary Todd. Soon after, they purchased a home in Springfield, Illinois. The Lincolns had four sons, but only one lived past the age of 19.

In 1846, Lincoln was elected to the United States Congress, where he served one term in the House of Representatives. Fourteen years later, he was elected President of the United States. Lincoln is the only President to own a patent for an invention. In 1849 he patented a device for lifting boats up over shallow places in rivers. Lincoln was also presented with several honorary degrees during the time of the Civil War.

As respected and honored as President Lincoln was, Mrs. Lincoln was not very popular in Washington. She came from a Southern family, and four of her brothers were in the Confederate army. Some people feared Mary Lincoln was a Confederate spy.

______ 1 The Lincolns had four children.

______ 2 Mrs. Lincoln was well liked in Washington.

______ 3 Mrs. Lincoln had brothers in the Confederate army.

______ 4 Lincoln never owned a home of his own.

______ 5 Lincoln received several honorary degrees.

______ 6 Many presidents had inventions that they patented.

______ 7 Lincoln went to school for many years.

______ 8 Lincoln was elected to the United States Senate.

Name ______________________ Date ____________

MAP AND GLOBE SKILLS

Compare Maps and Scales

Directions **Look at the maps below, and then answer the questions on the facing page.**

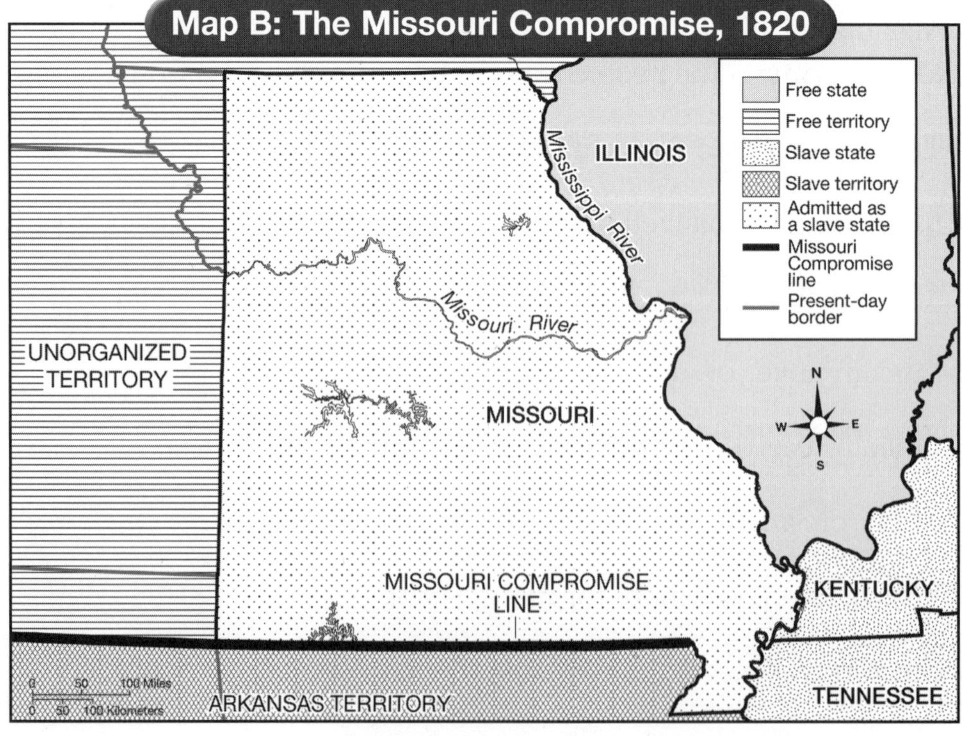

(continued)

Use after reading Chapter 12, Skill Lesson, pages 456–457.

Name ______________________________ Date ______________

Directions **Use the maps on page 116 to answer the questions below.**

1. Which map would be used to compare the size of Missouri to the size of Maine?

   ____

2. Which map would be used to determine the length of the border between Missouri and Kentucky? ______________________________

3. How many slave states were there at the time of the Missouri Compromise?

   ____

4. Was there more free territory or slave territory reserved?

   ____

5. Which state entered the Union at the same time as Missouri?

   ____

6. How many free states were there at the time of the Missouri Compromise?

   ____

Directions **Compare the two maps. Write *A* in the answer blank if Map A is more useful, and *B* if Map B is more useful.**

______ 7. Determine the length of the part of the Mississippi River that forms a Missouri border.

______ 8. Determine whether the free or slave states had the largest land area.

______ 9. Determine the length of the part of the Missouri River that flows from the eastern border to the western border of Missouri.

______ 10. Determine the number of miles of border separating the free states and the slave states.

Name ______________________ Date ____________

Civil War

Directions **In the box provided, write a brief paragraph to explain why each item on the left was important to the Civil War.**

EVENT	IMPORTANT BECAUSE
The Battle of Bull Run	
Anaconda Plan	
The Battle of Antietam	
The Emancipation Proclamation	

Use after reading Chapter 12, Lesson 4, pages 458–464.

Name ______________________ Date ____________

The Road to Union Victory

Directions **Place the Civil War events in chronological order by numbering the locations on the time line.**

1. Much of Atlanta burns to the ground after being captured by the Union army.
2. The Confederate army wins the Battle of Chancellorsville, and heads north towards Gettysburg.
3. The Union victory at the Battle of Gettysburg cripples the Confederate army.
4. General Robert E. Lee surrenders at Appomattox Courthouse, Virginia.
5. Lincoln gives the Gettysburg Address to inspire the nation and Union soldiers.
6. The Battle of Vicksburg gives the Union control of the Mississippi River.

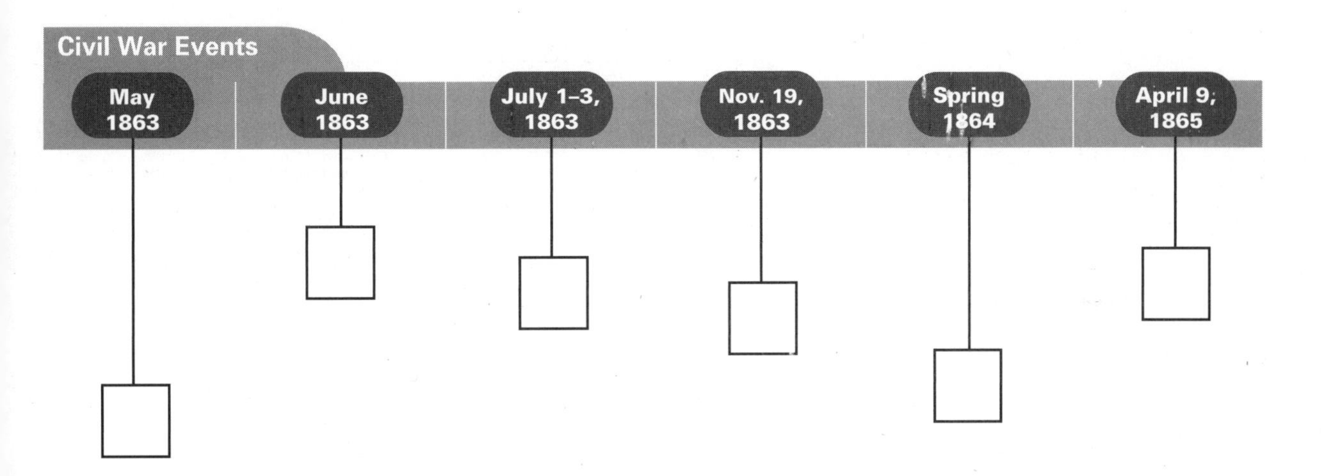

Name ______________________ Date ______________

Important Leaders and Battles of the Civil War

Directions Complete this graphic organizer by categorizing important leaders and battles of the Civil War.

UNION ARMY

IMPORTANT LEADERS

1. Abraham Lincoln
2. ______________________
3. ______________________

IMPORTANT VICTORIES

1. Battle of Gettysburg
2. ______________________
3. ______________________

CONFEDERATE ARMY

IMPORTANT LEADERS

1. Jefferson Davis
2. ______________________
3. ______________________

IMPORTANT VICTORIES

1. Victory at Fort Sumter
2. ______________________
3. ______________________

Use after reading Chapter 12, pages 435–471.

Name ______________________ Date ______________

Test Preparation

Directions **Read each question and choose the best answer. Then fill in the circle for the answer you have chosen. Be sure to fill in the circle completely.**

1. Who was one of the men who persuaded Congress to accept the Missouri Compromise?
   - Ⓐ John Calhoun
   - Ⓑ Daniel Webster
   - Ⓒ Henry Clay
   - Ⓓ Abraham Lincoln

2. Who defended the rights of both slaves and women?
   - Ⓕ Elizabeth Cady Stanton
   - Ⓖ Harriet Beecher Stowe
   - Ⓗ Clara Barton
   - Ⓙ Mary Todd Lincoln

3. Abraham Lincoln became well known through his debates with—
   - Ⓐ Henry Clay.
   - Ⓑ Stephen Douglas.
   - Ⓒ Jefferson Davis.
   - Ⓓ Major Robert Anderson.

4. The Union strategy to win the war by weakening the South was called the—
   - Ⓕ Join or Die Plan.
   - Ⓖ slash and burn policy.
   - Ⓗ King Cotton policy.
   - Ⓙ Anaconda Plan.

5. How did Abraham Lincoln honor the dead at Gettysburg?
   - Ⓐ He set up a memorial fund.
   - Ⓑ He had a monument built at the cemetery.
   - Ⓒ He gave a speech at the cemetery.
   - Ⓓ He sent the Vice President to the battlefield.

Name ______________________________ Date ______________

Reconstruction

Directions **Read the time line of events surrounding Reconstruction below. Then answer the questions that follow.**

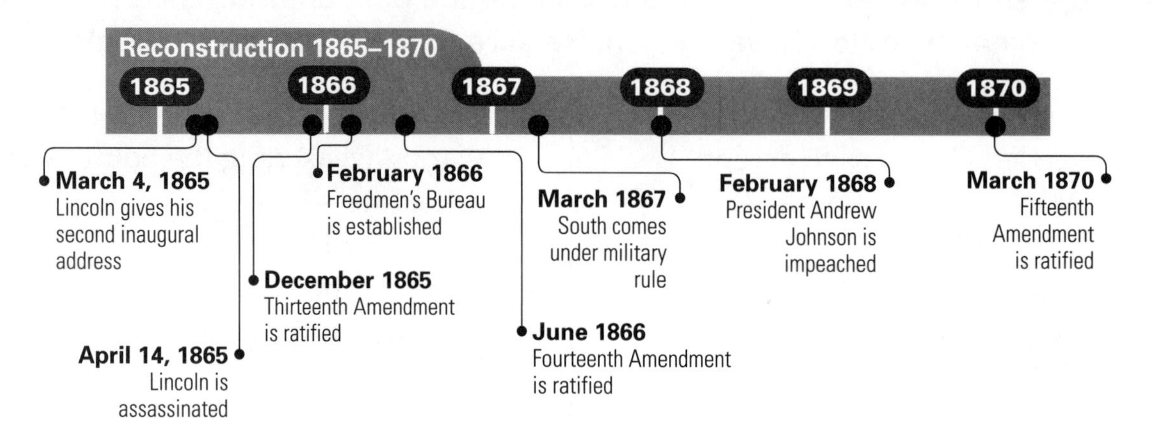

1. Was the Thirteenth Amendment ratified before or after President Lincoln gave his second inaugural address? ______________________________

2. What happened to President Abraham Lincoln on April 14, 1865?

____

____

3. About how many years passed between President Lincoln's assassination and President Johnson's impeachment? ______________________________

4. What two events shown on the time line both happened in the month of February? ______________________________

____

5. Was the Freedmen's Bureau established before or after the South came under military rule? ______________________________

____

6. How many constitutional amendments were passed between 1865 and 1870?

____

Use after reading Chapter 13, Lesson 1, pages 476–480.

Name ______________________ Date ______________

The South After the War

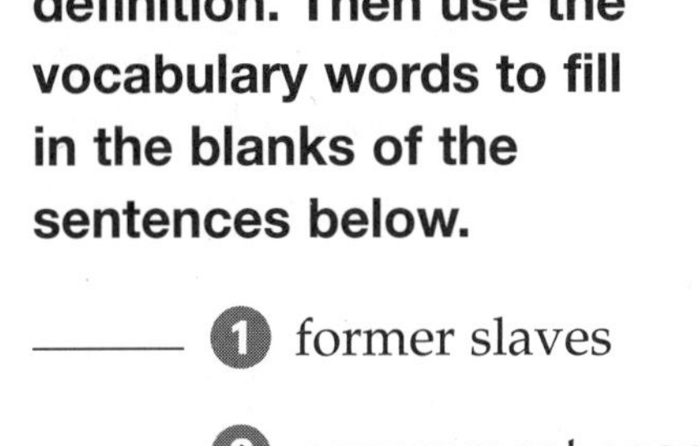

Directions **Match each vocabulary word with its definition. Then use the vocabulary words to fill in the blanks of the sentences below.**

_____ 1 former slaves

_____ 2 government agency

_____ 3 the practice of paying farm workers in harvested crops

_____ 4 Northerners who went South during Reconstruction

_____ 5 a method of voting in which no one knows for whom you voted

_____ 6 separation of people based on race

A. segregation

B. bureau

C. secret ballot

D. freedmen

E. carpetbaggers

F. sharecropping

7 The ______________________ is one of the most important parts of a fair election.

8 There are still many ______________________ in the United States government.

9 Life was hard for the ______________________ after the Civil War since few of them had enough money to buy their own land.

10 ______________________ were given their name because of the suitcases many of them used to carry their belongings.

11 The practice of ______________________ kept people apart in most public places.

12 Under the ______________________ system most farmworkers found it difficult to make a living.

Name ______________________ Date ______________

Settling the Last Frontier

Directions **Study the map below.**

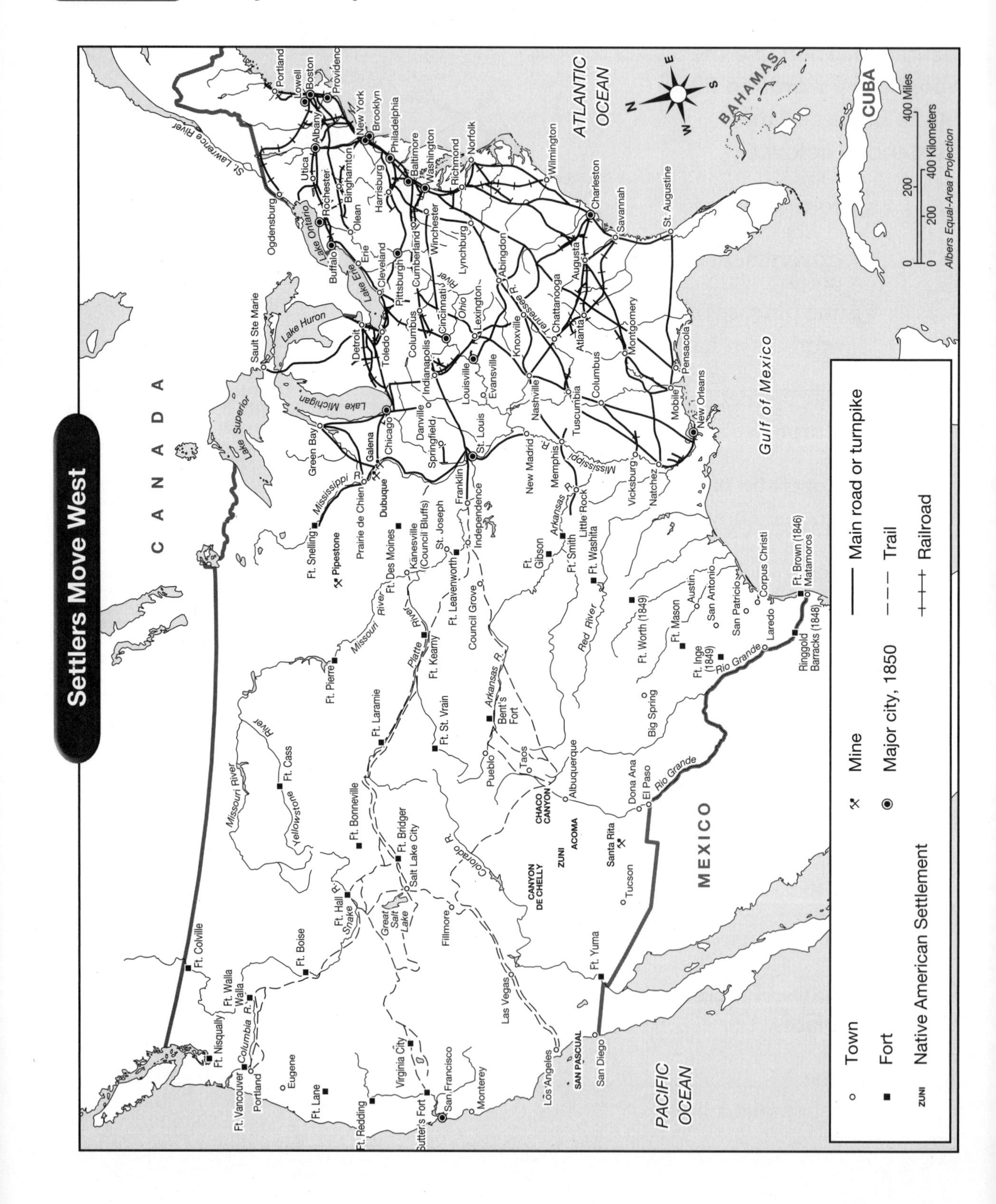

(continued)

Use after reading Chapter 13, Lesson 3, pages 486–491.

Name ______________________ Date ____________

Directions **Use the map and key on the preceding page to help you answer the questions. Write your answers in the blanks provided.**

1. In what part of the country were most railroads located?

   ____

2. What Texas fort was the farthest west? ______________________

3. In what parts of the country were most forts located? ______________________

   ____

4. Could you travel by railroad from St. Louis, Missouri, to Salt Lake City?

   ____

5. How might you travel from Norfolk, Virginia, to Wilmington, North Carolina?

   ____

6. Find the area that represents your state on the map. How settled was it? What might life have been like for the settlers who lived there?

   ____

   ____

   ____

   ____

   ____

Name ______________________ Date ____________

CHART AND GRAPH SKILLS

Use a Climograph

Directions **Look at the climograph of Austin, Texas, below. Then answer the questions on the blanks provided.**

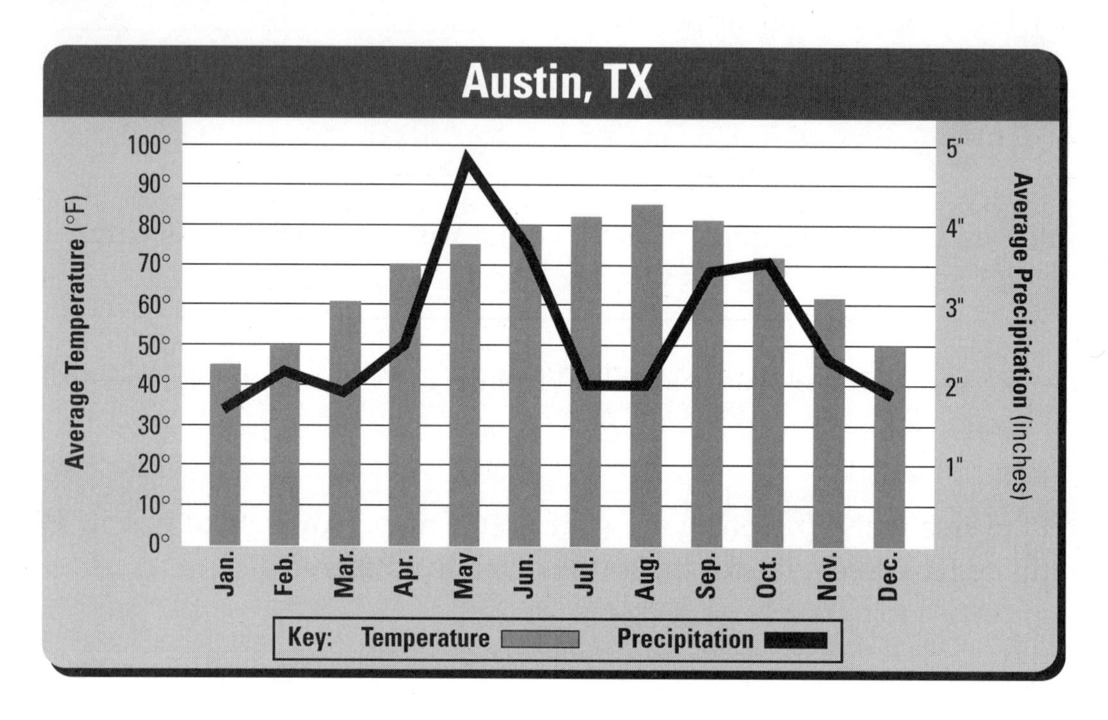

(continued)

Use after reading Chapter 13, Skill Lesson, pages 492–493.

Name ______________________ Date ____________

1. What is the average temperature in Austin in July? ____________

2. What is the average precipitation in October? ____________

3. Which three months are the driest? ____________

4. Which month is the coolest month? ____________

5. Which month is the warmest month? ____________

6. Which month gets the most precipitation? ____________

7. What do you observe about the months of July and August?

____

8. If you were driving cattle, what months do you think would be hardest on people and cattle? What hardships might you face during the drive?

____

____

____

____

Name ______________________ Date ____________

The Rise of New Industries

Directions **Read the passages below, and answer the questions that follow.**

In the 1800s the United States government made land grants to several railroad companies. More than 130 million acres were given to the Union Pacific, the Santa Fe, the Central and Southern Pacific, and the Northern Pacific railroads. In addition, western states gave the railroads 49 million acres. These land grants allowed the railroad industry to open new markets in the West for goods produced in the East.

One effect of the railroad boom was the need for stronger track. When the railroads were first built, the rails were made of iron. With the arrival of bigger and faster locomotives, however, these iron rails were not strong enough to withstand the weight of the new trains. A man named Henry Bessemer invented a way to make steel tracks strong enough for the larger locomotives. As a result, many companies were able to ship their products throughout the United States at a faster pace.

One company that used the new, faster trains to its advantage was Standard Oil. Founded by John D. Rockefeller in 1867, Standard Oil used the trains to ship oil all over the country. By 1882 Standard Oil controlled almost all of the oil refining and distribution in the United States.

1. Where did the railroad companies get the land on which they built the lines? ______________________

____

2. What effect did replacing iron rails with steel rails have on how United States companies could ship their products? ______________________

____

3. What company did John D. Rockefeller found in 1867? ______________________

____

4. What role do you think the railroads played in the growth of Standard Oil?

____

____

Use after reading Chapter 13, Lesson 4, pages 494–499.

Name ______________________ Date ____________

A Changing People

Directions **Read the passage below and answer the questions that follow.**

Irving Berlin's father was a cantor, a person who sings at religious services in Jewish synagogues. Perhaps it was his father's music that caused Berlin to be interested in writing songs. When he was in the Army during World War I, Berlin wrote a musical show. He later won both the United States Army's Award of Merit and a congressional medal for his songs. One of his most popular songs is "God Bless America."

Although Sophia Alice Callahan lived to be only 26 years old, she wrote an important novel. *Wynema: A Child of the Forest* is thought to be the first novel written by a Native American woman. Callahan's father was one-eighth Creek Indian. The novel has two major characters, Wynema and a Methodist teacher named Genevieve, who try to overcome prejudice against both Indians and women in the late nineteenth century.

Hiram Fong graduated from Harvard Law School before he returned to his native Hawaii to practice law. Hawaii at that time was still a territory. Fong served in the territorial legislature from 1938 to 1954. When Hawaii became a state, he was elected to the United States Senate. He served in the Senate from 1959 until 1977.

African American artist Jacob Lawrence did a 63-painting series on the lives of Harriet Tubman and Frederick Douglass. He studied painting in the Harlem section of New York City. During the depression, Lawrence worked for a federal project. This gave him enough money to be able to paint *Migration*, a series of 60 panels showing the movement of African Americans from the South to the North.

1. Explain what all the people in the passage have in common.

____

____

____

2. Who might have influenced Irving Berlin's interest in music?

____

3. How did Hiram Fong serve his homeland? ______________________

____

4. What two series of paintings were created by Jacob Lawrence?

____

____

Name ______________________ Date ____________

Abraham Lincoln and Reconstruction

Directions **Complete this graphic organizer by describing different points of view about Reconstruction.**

WHO SAID IT	WHAT WAS SAID	WHY IT WAS SAID	POINT OF VIEW
____________	"With malice toward none, with charity for all, with firmness in the right as God gives us to see the right, let us strive on to finish the work we are in, to bind up the nation's wounds..."	Because the country had been torn apart by the Civil War	____________

WHO SAID IT	WHAT WAS SAID	WHY IT WAS SAID	POINT OF VIEW
Mary Chesnut	"Lincoln—old Abe Lincoln—killed... I know this foul murder will bring down miseries on us."	____________	____________

Use after reading Chapter 13, pages 475–507.

• CHAPTER •

13

Name ______________________ Date ______________

Test Preparation

Directions **Read each question and choose the best answer. Then fill in the circle for the answer you have chosen. Be sure to fill in the circle completely.**

1. Which of the following was **not** a condition for a Southern state's readmission to the Union?
   - Ⓐ rewriting the state's constitution
   - Ⓑ giving slaves some of the land
   - Ⓒ ratifying the Thirteenth Amendment
   - Ⓓ ratifying the Fifteenth Amendment

2. The most important work of the Freedmen's Bureau was—
   - Ⓕ education.
   - Ⓖ running the courts.
   - Ⓗ helping people farm.
   - Ⓙ rebuilding homes.

3. Which of the following was **not** a problem for homesteaders?
   - Ⓐ drought
   - Ⓑ range wars
   - Ⓒ bitter cold and snow
   - Ⓓ land costs

4. The last of the transcontinental railroad was laid in—
   - Ⓕ Spokane, Washington.
   - Ⓖ Promontory, Utah.
   - Ⓗ Erie, Pennsylvania.
   - Ⓙ St. Louis, Missouri.

5. The term "new immigration" refers to—
   - Ⓐ people coming from Britain, Germany, and Ireland.
   - Ⓑ African Americans moving north.
   - Ⓒ people coming from Italy, Russia, and Greece.
   - Ⓓ people coming from South America.

Name ______________________________ Date ______________

Building an American Empire

Directions **Use the information below to complete the chart.**

- Americans set up a republic in 1893. The United States annexes the territory in 1898.
- Source of fish, timber, coal, copper, and gold
- Secretary of State William Seward buys the land from Russia in 1867.
- For producing cattle and sugar
- To link American ports on the Atlantic coast with those on the Pacific coast
- The United States supports a revolution against Colombia. In 1904, the United States begins a major building project.

Territory	How and When Territory Was Added	Reason for Acquiring Territory
Alaska		
Hawaii		
Panama Canal Zone		

(continued)

Use after reading Chapter 14, Lesson 1, pages 524–529.

Name ______________________________ Date ______________

Directions **Use the information from the table on the previous page and the map below to write a paragraph to convince someone that Alaska, Hawaii, or the Panama Canal Zone should be added to the United States.**

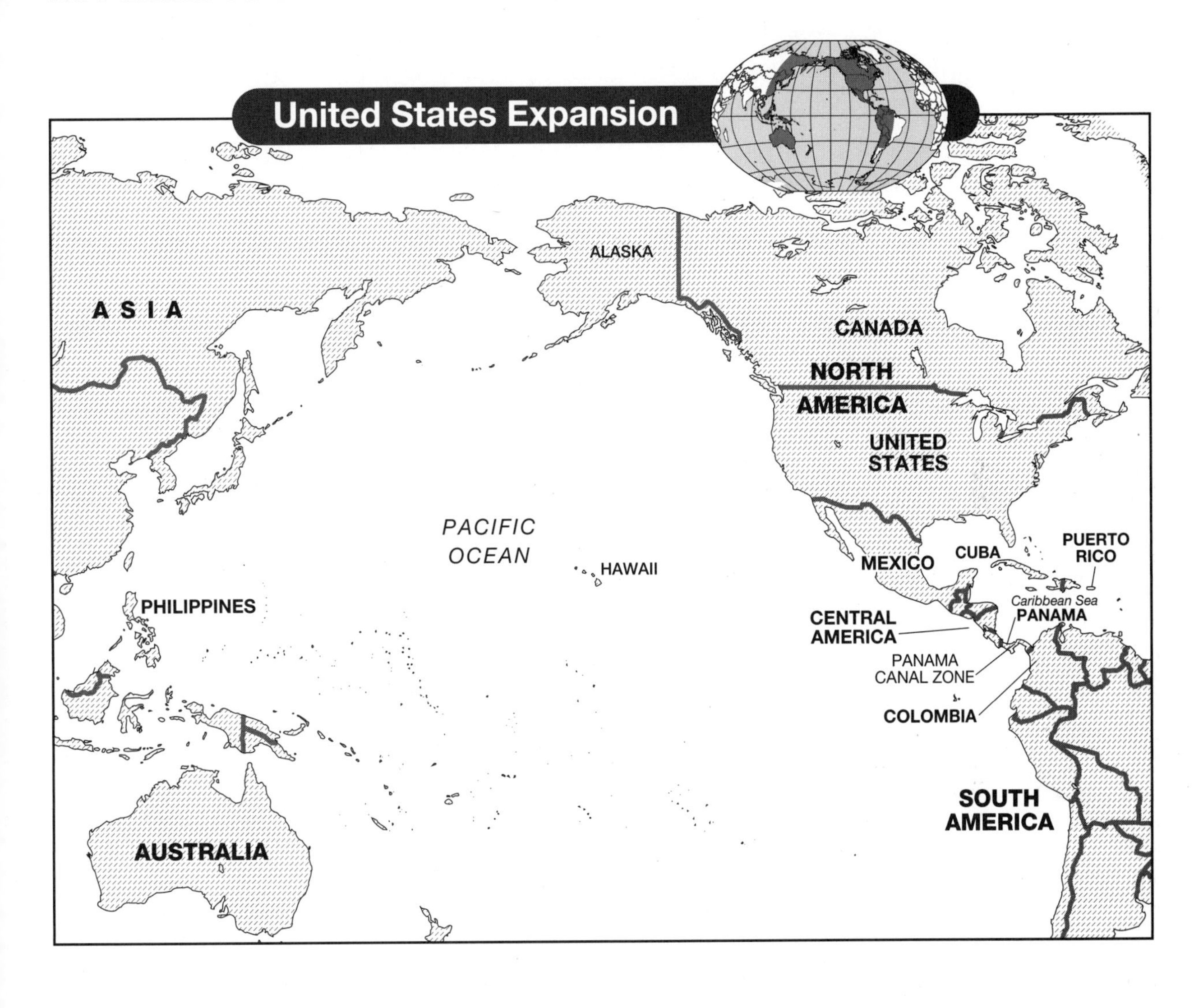

____

____

____

____

____

____

____

____

Name ______________________ Date ______________

MAP AND GLOBE SKILLS

Compare Map Projections

(continued)

Use after reading Chapter 14, Skill Lesson, pages 530–531.

Name ______________________________ Date ______________

Directions **Study the conformal projection and equal-area projection maps. For each statement below, put a check mark in the column for which the statement is true. Some statements will be true for both projections. All statements will be true for at least one projection.**

Conformal Projection	Equal-Area Projection	
______	______	1 Shows the nations of Europe in 1914
______	______	2 Shows the curved feature of Earth
______	______	3 Uses straight lines for all lines of latitude and longitude
______	______	4 Shows all lines of latitude and longitude at right angles to each other
______	______	5 Shows national borders
______	______	6 Shows most of the Ottoman Empire
______	______	7 Uses a straight line for the prime meridian
______	______	8 Shows directions correctly
______	______	9 Shows parallels *not* intersecting
______	______	10 Shows correctly the sizes of nations compared with one another
______	______	11 Shows lines of latitude farther apart at the poles
______	______	12 Uses curved lines to show latitude
______	______	13 Uses straight lines to show longitude
______	______	14 Shows lines of longitude closer together toward the north pole
______	______	15 Shows all meridians the same distance apart
______	______	16 Changes the shapes of nations

Use after reading Chapter 14, Skill Lesson, pages 530–531.

Name ______________________________ Date ______________

Progressives and Reform

Directions **Identify which group was responsible for making each of the reforms listed in the Word Bank below. Then write each reform in the correct section of the chart.**

end boss rule	National Association for the Advancement of Colored People	national parks	Square Deal
Interstate Commerce Commission	National League of Women Voters	National Urban League	support for injured workers
limit child labor		Pure Food and Drug Act	ten-hour workday
merit system		settlement houses	women's suffrage
			Wisconsin Idea

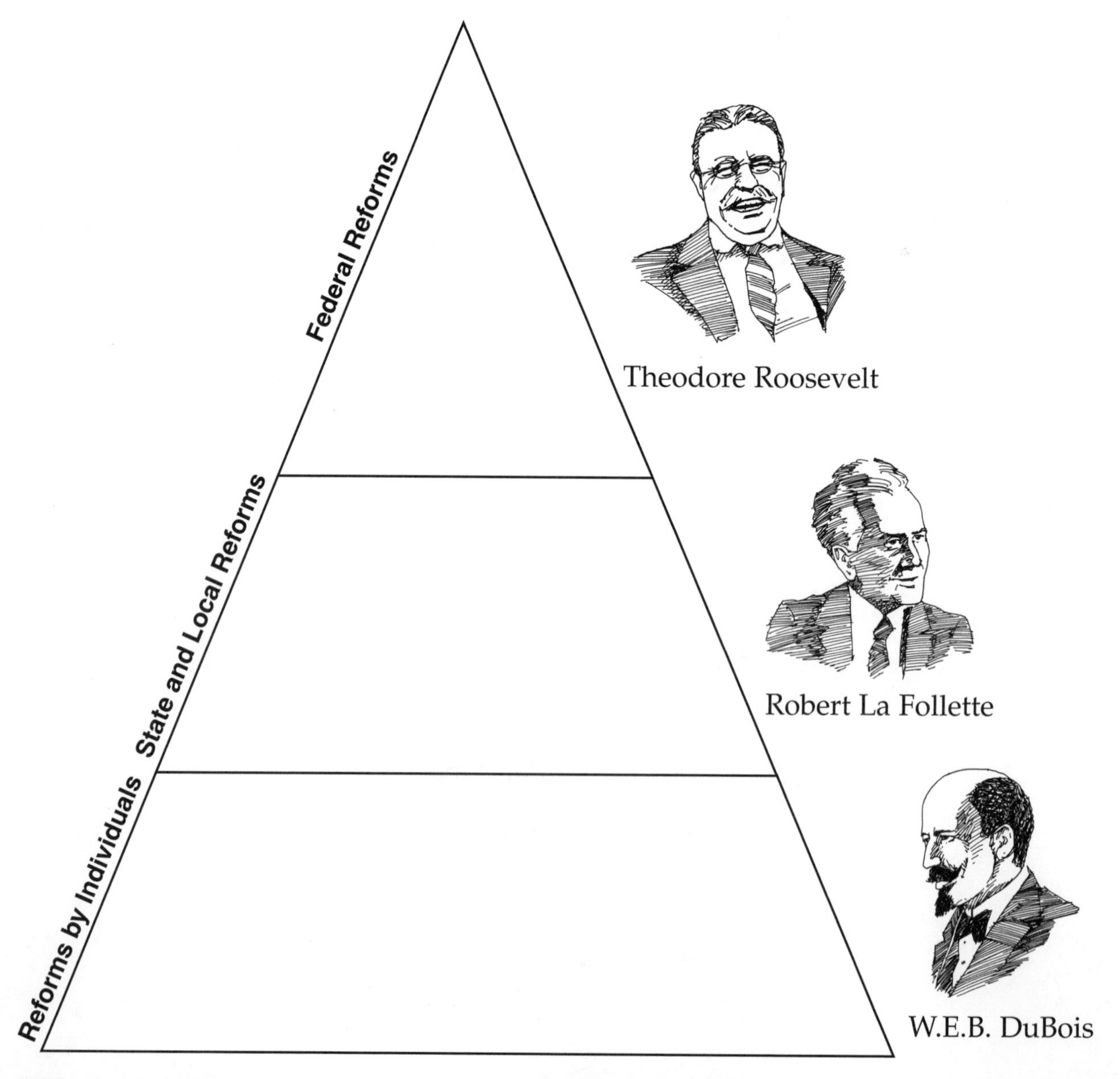

Theodore Roosevelt

Robert La Follette

W.E.B. DuBois

Use after reading Chapter 14, Lesson 2, pages 532–536.

Name ______________________ Date ______________

The Great War

Directions **Write a short story about an American family during World War I. Some topics that you may want to feature in your story include worries about German U-boats, concerns about the draft, fighting to make the world "safe for democracy," and thoughts about a family member serving overseas. You may also want to describe how the war has changed the lives of women and African Americans.**

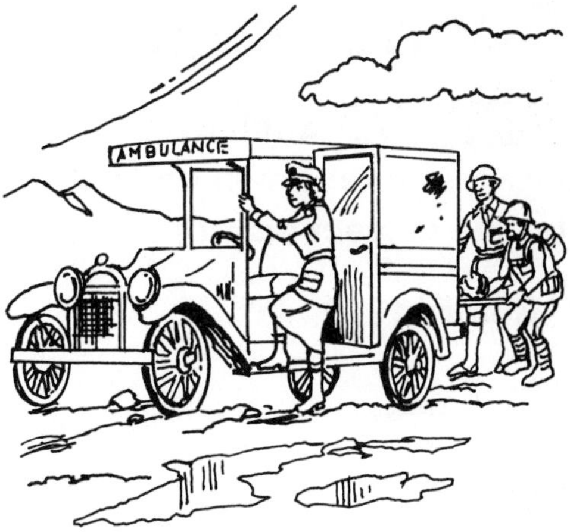

Use after reading Chapter 14, Lesson 3, pages 537–541.

Name ______________________ Date ____________

Boom Times and Depression

Directions **Each event listed below occurred either before or after the stock market crash on October 29, 1929. Write the number of each event on the correct side of the time line below.**

Before 1929 **After 1929**

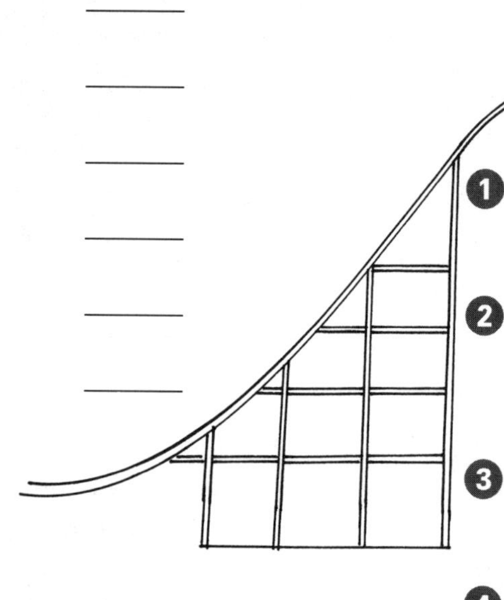

1. The size of the federal government is greatly increased.
2. African American artists, musicians, and writers launch the Harlem Renaissance.
3. Americans elect Franklin Roosevelt for his first term as President.
4. Automobiles become affordable and popular.
5. Charles Lindbergh flies across the Atlantic in the *Spirit of St. Louis.*
6. Congress sets up the Tennessee Valley Authority.
7. For the first time in United States history, more people live in cities than on farms.
8. Moviegoers see the first "talkies."
9. President Roosevelt announces the New Deal.
10. The number of United States commercial radio stations tops 800.
11. Jazz becomes a popular form of music.
12. American farmers are hurt by low crop prices.

Use after reading Chapter 14, Lesson 4, pages 542–549.

Name ______________________ Date ____________

The Great Depression

Directions **Complete this graphic organizer by making inferences about the Great Depression.**

FACT		INFERENCE
On October 29, 1929, the stock market crashed.	↗	______
FACT		
______	↘	

FACT		INFERENCE
______	↗	Because manufacturers could not sell their products, factories shut down and more people lost their jobs.
FACT		
______	↘	

· CHAPTER ·

14

Name ____________________ Date __________

Test Preparation

Directions **Read each question and choose the best answer. Then fill in the circle for the answer you have chosen. Be sure to fill in the circle completely.**

1. Which area did the United States gain as a result of the Spanish-American War?
   - Ⓐ Alaska
   - Ⓑ Hawaii
   - Ⓒ Puerto Rico
   - Ⓓ Panama Canal

2. One of the main goals of the progressives was to—
   - Ⓕ make peace with Germany.
   - Ⓖ overcome the Great Depression.
   - Ⓗ improve state and local government.
   - Ⓙ expand the territory of the United States.

3. Which best describes the Great Migration?
   - Ⓐ Many Germans moved to the United States during the 1920s, after World War I.
   - Ⓑ Many African Americans moved to northern cities, especially during World War I.
   - Ⓒ Many immigrants left cities to find work in the suburbs during the Great Depression.
   - Ⓓ Many workers left the United States after losing their jobs during the Great Depression.

4. Langston Hughes was a—
   - Ⓕ scientist who helped southern farmers.
   - Ⓖ American military leader during World War I.
   - Ⓗ government official who purchased Alaska.
   - Ⓙ well-known poet of the Harlem Renaissance.

5. The New Deal was Franklin D. Roosevelt's plan to—
   - Ⓐ help immigrants adjust to life in the United States.
   - Ⓑ organize the American effort to build the Panama Canal.
   - Ⓒ support the Allies against the Central Powers in World War I.
   - Ⓓ put Americans back to work and end the Great Depression.

Use after reading Chapter 14, pages 522–551.

Name ______________________ Date ______________

World War II Begins

Directions **Below is a list of causes and effects related to World War II. Write each cause and effect in the appropriate place on the chart.**

- Germany invades Poland in 1939.
- Dictators rise to power in Germany, Italy, Spain, and the Soviet Union.
- Japan attacks Pearl Harbor.
- The Soviet Union joins with Britain and France to fight the Axis Powers.

CAUSE	EFFECT
World War I and the economic depression of the 1930s bring hard times to many countries around the world.	______________________
______________________	**The United States declares war on Japan.**
______________________	**France and Britain declare war on Germany, and World War II begins.**
Germany invades the Soviet Union.	______________________

Name ______________________ Date ____________

READING SKILLS

Predict a Historical Outcome

Directions **The flow chart below lists the steps for predicting a likely outcome. Follow the steps to predict the effects of the end of World War II on the United States economy.**

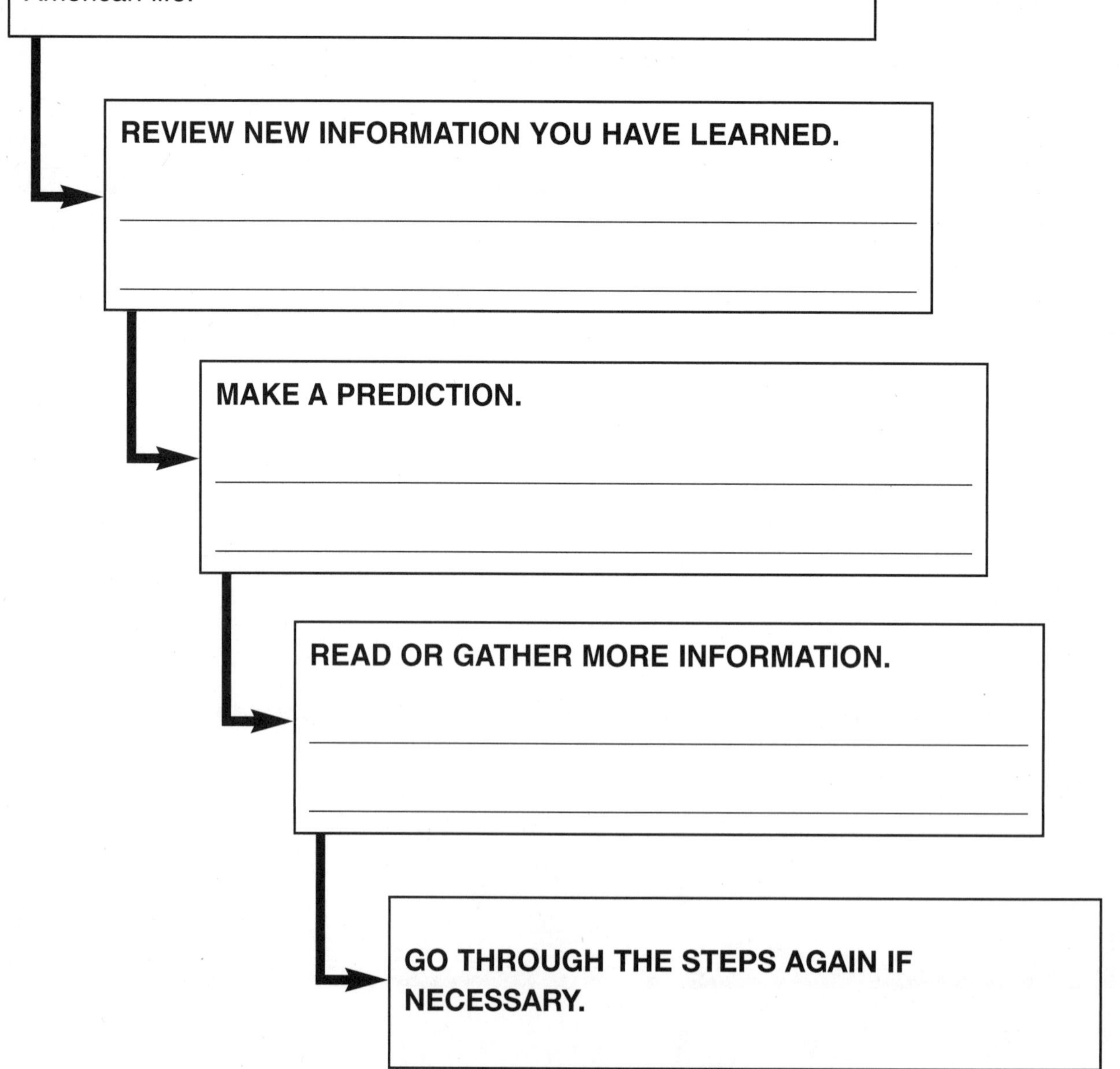

THINK ABOUT WHAT YOU ALREADY KNOW.

At the end of World War I, the United States economy prospered. In the years that followed, new consumer products appeared on the market, and new forms of entertainment became part of American life.

REVIEW NEW INFORMATION YOU HAVE LEARNED.

____

____

MAKE A PREDICTION.

____

____

READ OR GATHER MORE INFORMATION.

____

____

GO THROUGH THE STEPS AGAIN IF NECESSARY.

Use after reading Chapter 15, Skill Lesson, page 559.

Name ______________________ Date ______________

Americans and the War

Directions **During World War II Americans at home were told to "Use it up, wear it out, make it do, or do without." Write a paragraph that explains the meaning of this motto and the reasons Americans were encouraged to do this during the war.**

____

____

____

____

____

____

____

____

____

____

Name ______________________ Date ______________

CITIZENSHIP SKILLS

Make Economic Choices

Directions **Imagine you have $25 to spend. You must choose between a savings bond which will increase in value after a certain number of years or one of two items you would like to buy. Complete the graphic organizer below to help you make an economic choice.**

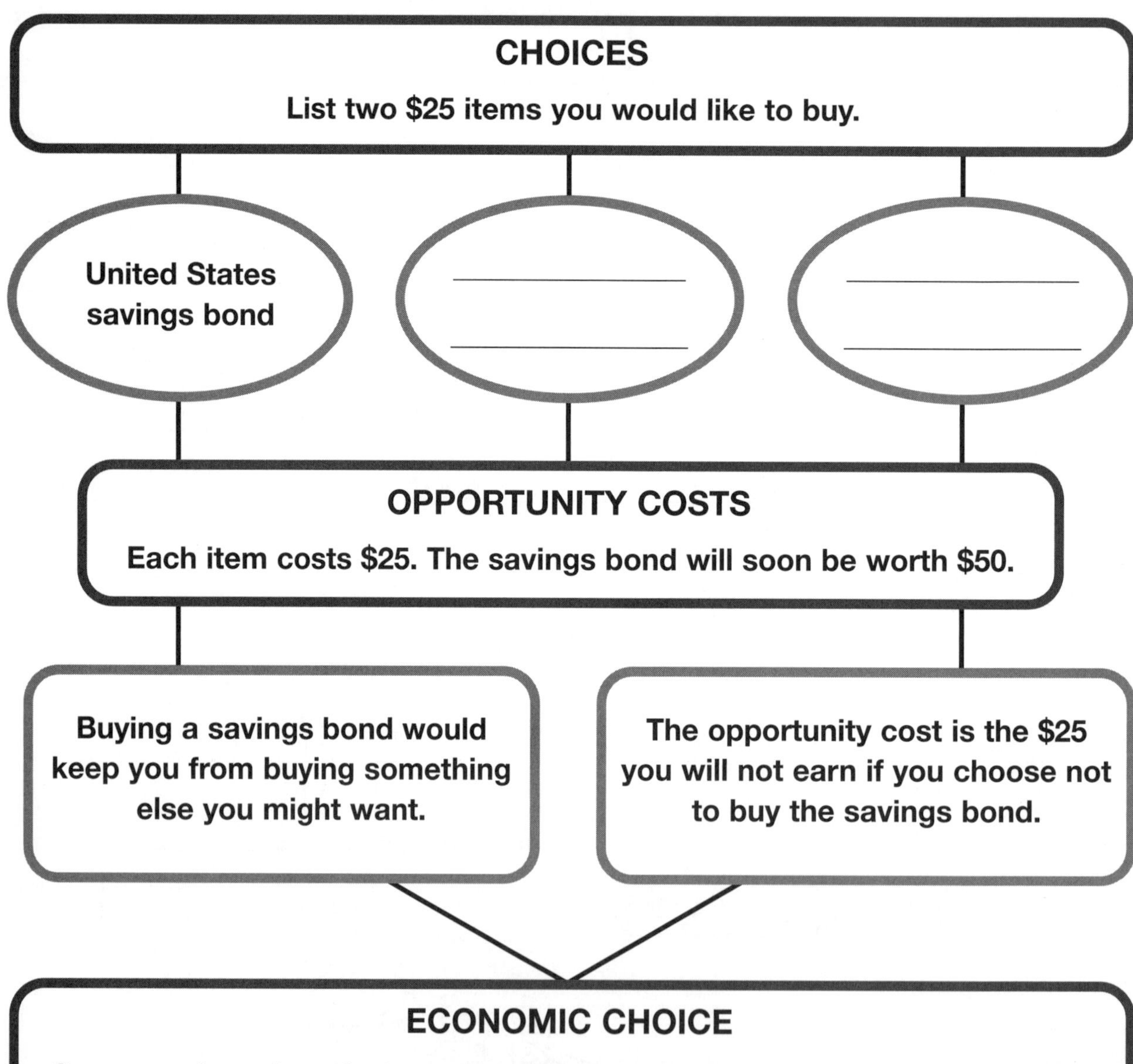

Use after reading Chapter 15, Skill Lesson, page 564.

Name ______________________ Date ____________

Winning the War

Directions **Use the terms below to solve the crossword puzzle.**

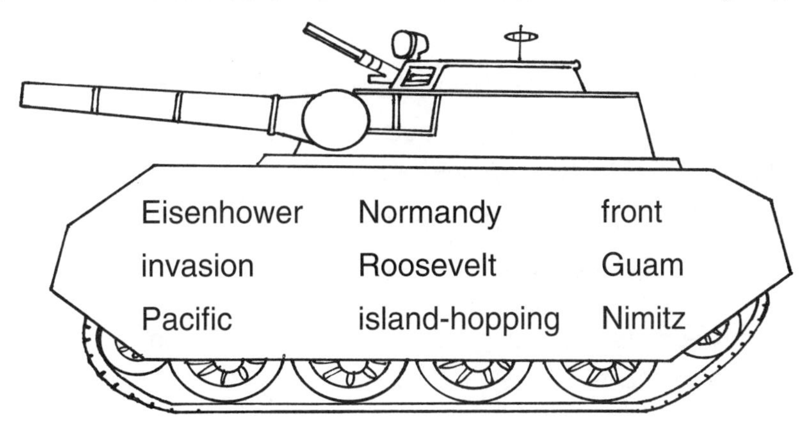

Across

3. Ocean that surrounds Hawaii
4. D day landing site
7. Allies' plan for defeating Japan

Down

1. Action taken by Allies on D day
2. Commander of Allied troops in Europe
4. American admiral in the Pacific
5. President of the United States during most of World War II
6. Battle line
8. Important Pacific island captured by Allied troops

Name ______________________________ Date ______________

CHART AND GRAPH SKILLS

Read Parallel Time Lines

Directions **Find the year each of the following events took place. Write the year in the space provided. Then, if the event occurred in the United States, write the letter of the event at the appropriate date below the *Events at Home* time line. Write the letters of all the events that occurred outside the United States at the appropriate date below the *Events Overseas* time line.**

______ **A.** Allies push Germany out of North Africa.

______ **B.** Japan invades Indochina.

______ **C.** American troops capture Rome.

______ **D.** President Roosevelt dies.

______ **E.** President Roosevelt gives the "Date of Infamy" speech.

______ **F.** American factories produce almost 86,000 aircraft.

______ **G.** Germany surrenders.

______ **H.** Germany invades Poland.

______ **I.** Japanese Americans are forced to move to relocation camps.

______ **J.** Allies launch D day invasion.

______ **K.** Americans elect Franklin D. Roosevelt for a fourth term as President.

______ **L.** Japan surrenders.

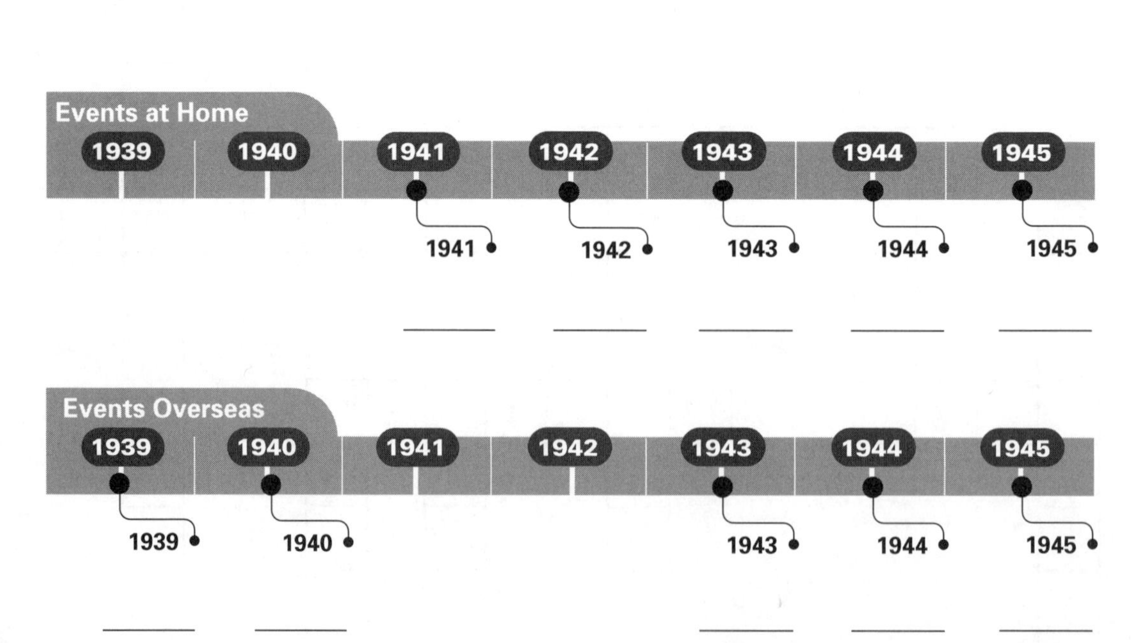

Use after reading Chapter 15, Skill Lesson, pages 570–571.

Name ______________________ Date ______________

The Effects of War

Directions **Write each effect of World War II in the appropriate column of the table below.**

- Germany's land is divided among Britain, France, the Soviet Union, and the United States.
- Nazi leaders are tried for their crimes at Nuremberg.
- More than 12 million people die in Nazi concentration camps; about half are European Jews.
- The Cold War begins.
- Europe and Japan begin rebuilding cities destroyed in the war.
- Representatives from 50 countries form the United Nations.
- The Soviet Union sets up communist governments in Eastern Europe.
- The United States introduces the Marshall Plan.

Effects of World War II		
The Holocaust	**Plans for Peace**	**A Changed World**

Use after reading Chapter 15, Lesson 4, pages 572–575.

Name ______________________ Date ____________

World War II and the United States

Directions **Complete this graphic organizer by determining the causes and effects of the involvement of the United States in World War II.**

CAUSE
The Japanese attack Pearl Harbor.

EFFECT	EFFECT	EFFECT
19 American ships are sunk or damaged and 150 planes are destroyed.		

CAUSE
The United States joins the Allied forces.

EFFECT	EFFECT	EFFECT
15 million Americans serve in the armed forces during the war.		

Use after reading Chapter 15, pages 553–575.

· CHAPTER ·

15

Name ______________________ Date ______________

Test Preparation

Directions **Read each question and choose the best answer. Then fill in the circle for the answer you have chosen. Be sure to fill in the circle completely.**

1. Who became dictator of the Soviet Union in 1924?
   - Ⓐ Adolf Hitler
   - Ⓑ Josef Stalin
   - Ⓒ Francisco Franco
   - Ⓓ Benito Mussolini

2. By the end of 1941, Germany had taken over—
   - Ⓕ Pearl Harbor.
   - Ⓖ much of China.
   - Ⓗ much of Europe.
   - Ⓙ Britain and Canada.

3. During World War II, many American women held jobs as—
   - Ⓐ fighter pilots.
   - Ⓑ wheat farmers.
   - Ⓒ factory workers.
   - Ⓓ cattle ranchers.

4. What strategy did the Allies use to defeat Japan in the Pacific?
   - Ⓕ the Marshall Plan
   - Ⓖ *Blitzkrieg*
   - Ⓗ relocation
   - Ⓙ island-hopping

5. Why did the Soviet Union join the Allies?
   - Ⓐ Germany attempted an invasion of the Soviet Union.
   - Ⓑ Japan launched a surprise attack against the Soviet Union.
   - Ⓒ The Soviet Union wanted to support other communist nations.
   - Ⓓ The Allies offered the Soviet Union aid from the Marshall Plan.

Name ______________________________ Date ______________

The Early Years of the Cold War

Directions **In the space provided, write the year each of the following events took place. Then write the number of each event in the appropriate place on the time line.**

1. ________ Americans elect Dwight D. Eisenhower as President.
2. ________ China becomes a communist country.
3. ________ Congress sets up NASA.
4. ________ Cuba becomes a communist country.
5. ________ East Germany builds a wall to stop its citizens from leaving.
6. ________ Lyndon Johnson becomes President of the United States.
7. ________ North Korea invades South Korea.
8. ________ President Kennedy is assassinated.
9. ________ South Korea becomes a republic; North Korea becomes a communist country.
10. ________ The Soviet Union cuts Berlin off from West Germany.
11. ________ The Soviet Union launches *Sputnik,* the first space satellite.
12. ________ The United States blockades Cuba to force it to remove Soviet missiles.
13. ________ United States astronaut Neil Armstrong becomes the first human to walk on the moon.

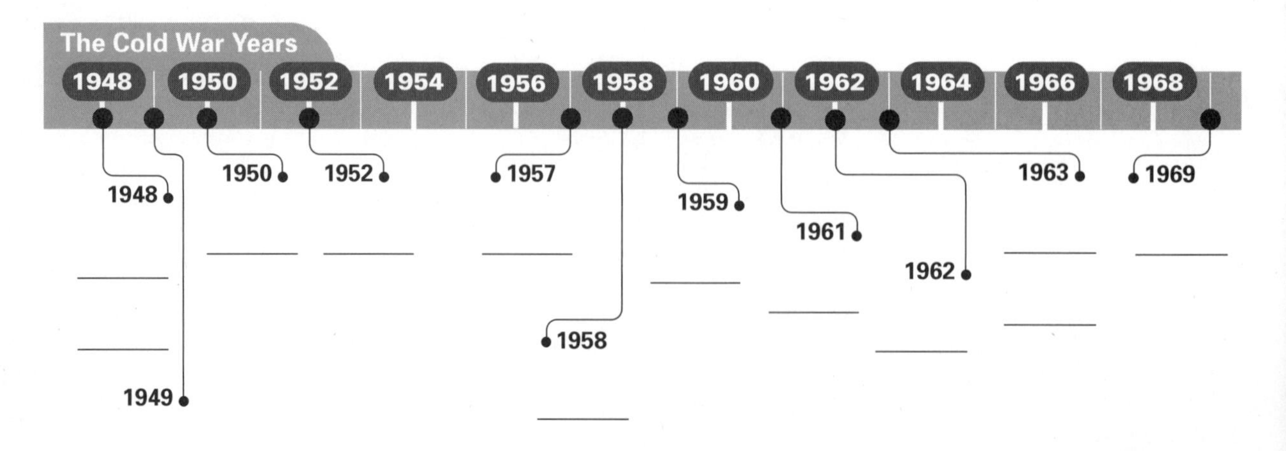

(continued)

Use after reading Chapter 16, Lesson 1, pages 580–584.

Name ______________________________ Date ______________

Directions **Use the information from the time line on the previous page to decide whether each statement below is true or false. If the statement is true, write a *T* next to the statement. If the statement is false, write an *F* and explain why the statement is false.**

_____ 14 North Korea became a communist country by following the example set by Cuba. ______________________________

____

_____ 15 Congress set up NASA in response to the Soviet blockade of Berlin.

____

____

_____ 16 President Johnson tried to stop China from becoming a communist country. ______________________________

____

_____ 17 The United States was the first nation to land a person on the moon.

____

____

_____ 18 The Soviet Union launched *Sputnik* to force President Kennedy to back down during the Cuban Missile Crisis. ______________________________

____

Name ________________________________ Date ______________

Working for Equal Rights

Directions **Use the information below to complete the chart.**

- Thurgood Marshall
- This person's refusal to give up a seat on a segregated bus led the United States Supreme Court to rule that public transportation could no longer be segregated.
- This leader fought for the rights of migrant farm workers and helped start a group that became the United Farm Workers.
- Malcolm X
- Cesar Chavez
- This winner of the Nobel Peace Prize helped lead the Montgomery bus boycott, encouraged people to use nonviolent ways to end segregation, and led a famous civil rights march in Washington, D.C.

Civil Rights Activist	Notable Ideas/Accomplishments
	This leader led a nationwide boycott of California grapes to convince grape growers to improve the pay and conditions for migrant workers.
Dolores Huerta	
Martin Luther King, Jr.	
	This lawyer argued and won the case *Brown v. Board of Education of Topeka,* which resulted in a United States Supreme Court ruling that public schools could no longer be segregated.
Rosa Parks	
	This civil rights leader at first spoke in favor of segregation, but later talked about racial cooperation.

Use after reading Chapter 16, Lesson 2, pages 585–589.

Name ______________________ Date ______________

The Cold War Continues

Directions **Below is a list of causes and effects related to the Vietnam War. Write each item from the list in the appropriate box on the cause-and-effect chart.**

Bombing does not stop North Vietnam from supporting Vietcong

President Nixon signs cease-fire

President Johnson orders bombing of North Vietnam

United States economy suffers

United States wants to stop spread of communism

President Nixon wants to withdraw from Vietnam, but does not want communists to take over South Vietnam

South Vietnam surrenders

United States blockades North Vietnam and increases bombing

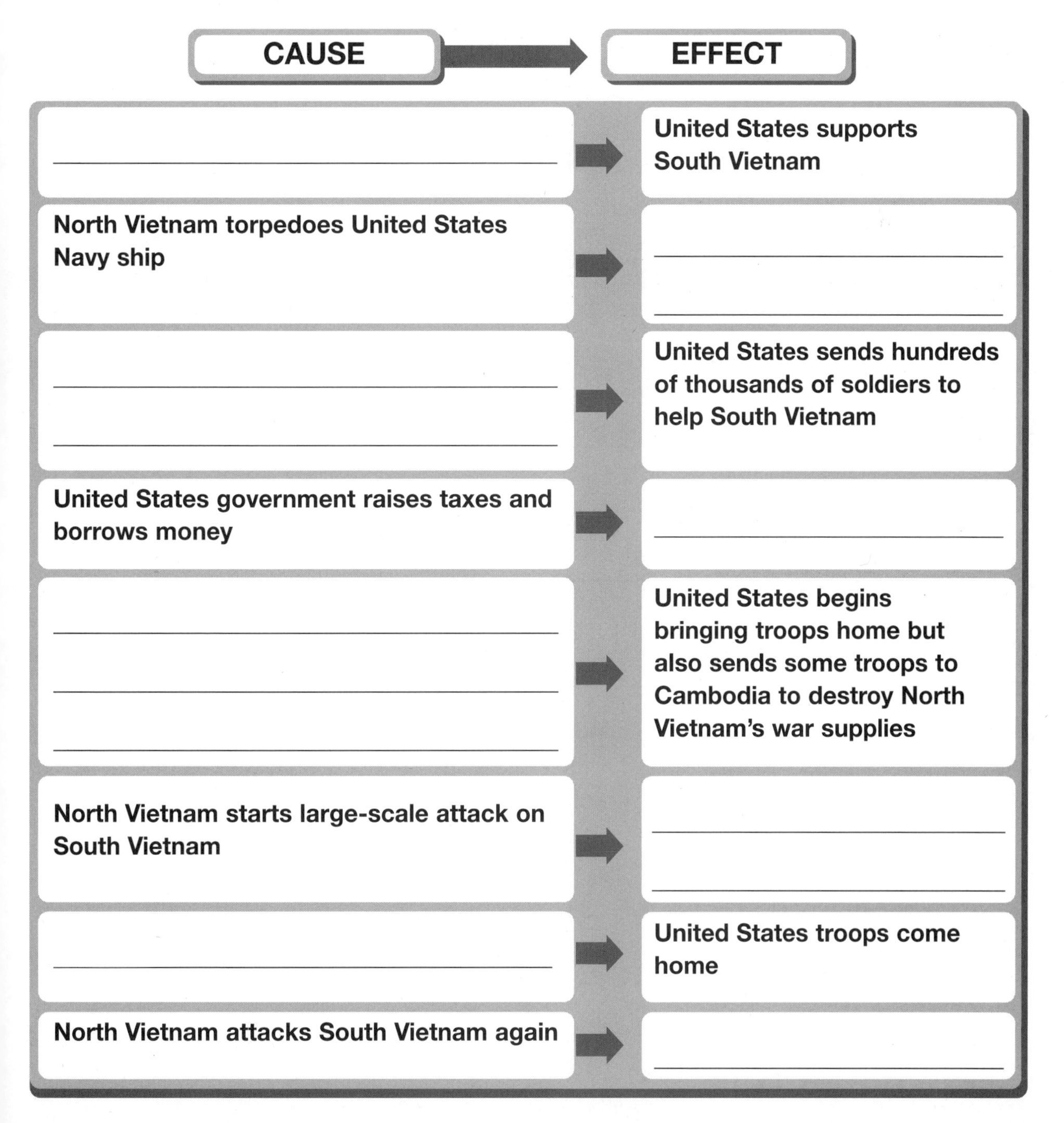

CAUSE	EFFECT
______________	United States supports South Vietnam
North Vietnam torpedoes United States Navy ship	______________
______________	United States sends hundreds of thousands of soldiers to help South Vietnam
United States government raises taxes and borrows money	______________
______________	United States begins bringing troops home but also sends some troops to Cambodia to destroy North Vietnam's war supplies
North Vietnam starts large-scale attack on South Vietnam	______________
______________	United States troops come home
North Vietnam attacks South Vietnam again	______________

Use after reading Chapter 16, Lesson 3, pages 590–593.

Name ______________________ Date ______________

A World of Change

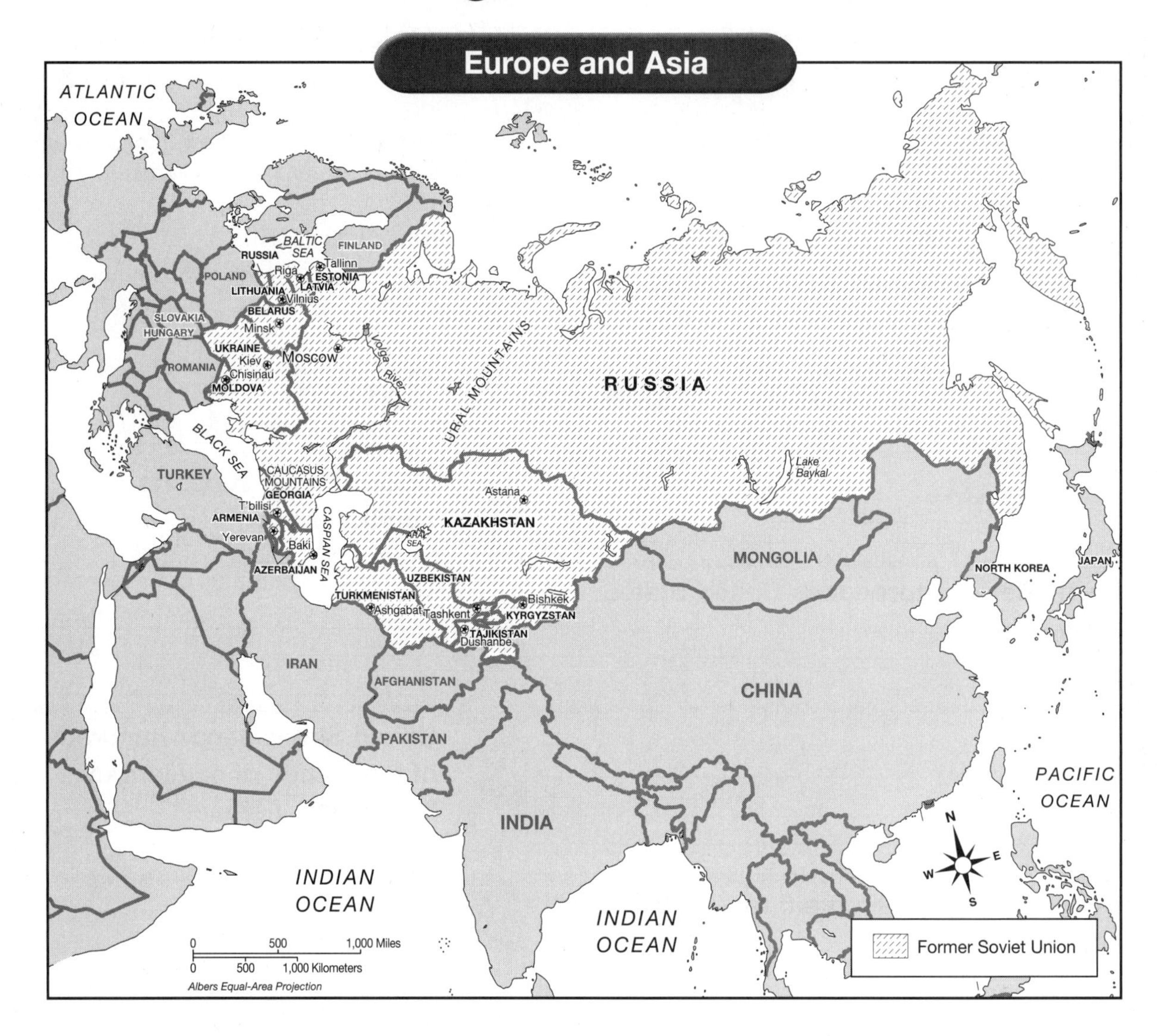

(continued)

Use after reading Chapter 16, Lesson 4, pages 596–601.

Name ______________________ Date ____________

Directions **Study the map on page 154, and answer the questions below.**

1. When the Soviet Union broke up, how many independent countries were formed? ______________________

2. Which of these independent countries is the largest? ______________________

3. Which of these independent countries reaches the farthest south?

____

4. Which of these independent countries share a border with China?

____

5. Which of these independent countries share a border with Afghanistan?

____

6. Which of these independent countries have access to the Black Sea?

____

7. Which body of water is at the southern end of the Volga River?

____

8. What is the capital of Uzbekistan? ______________________

9. Of the countries that were formerly part of the Soviet Union, which has the northernmost capital? ______________________

10. Which mountains are on the northern border of the Republic of Georgia?

____

Name ______________________ Date ____________

MAP AND GLOBE SKILLS
Read a Population Map

Directions **Study the map, and answer the questions below.**

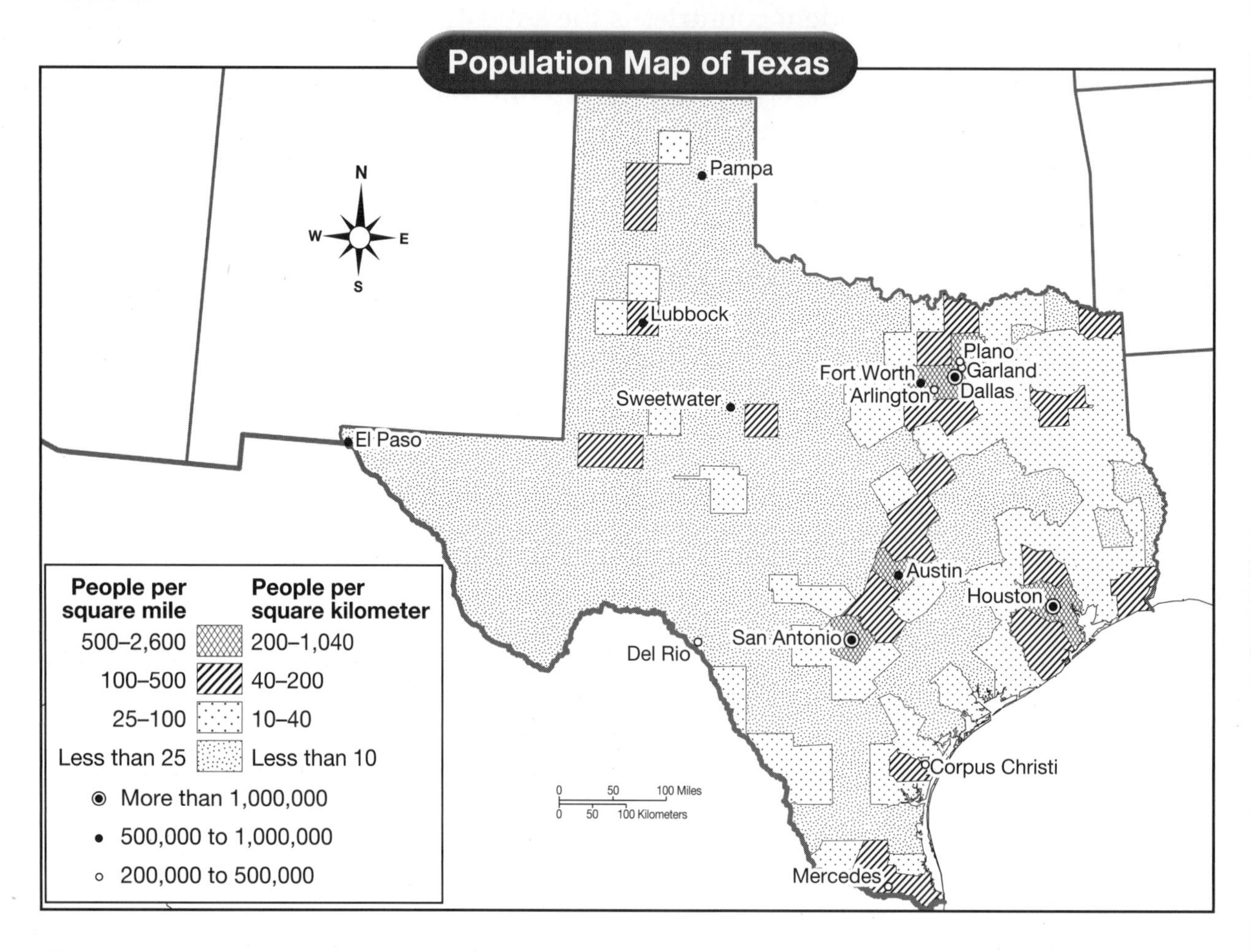

1. About how many people per square mile live in El Paso?

____

2. About how many people per square mile live in Corpus Christi?

____

3. Do more people live in Plano or in Dallas? ____________________

4. Which is more populated, East Texas or West Texas? ____________________

(continued)

Use after reading Chapter 16, Skill Lesson, pages 602–603.

Name ______________________________ Date ______________

Population density is the number of people per unit of area, such as "100 people per square mile." Population density describes how crowded an area is. To calculate population density, divide the total number of people by the total area of land. For example, the United States has a population of 272,639,608 and is 3,717,796 square miles in area.

Population ÷ Area = Population Density
272,639,608 ÷ 3,717,796 = about 73 people per square mile

To do this on a calculator:

enter 2 7 2 6 3 9 6 0 8 press ÷ enter 3 7 1 7 7 9 6 press =

Directions **Calculate the population densities of the nations listed below.**

5. Australia's population is 18,783,551 people, and its area is 2,967,900 square miles.

______________ ÷ ______________ = ____________ people per square mile
(population) *(area)* *(population density)*

6. The United Kingdom's population is 59,113,439 people, and its area is 94,500 square miles.

______________ ÷ ______________ = ____________ people per square mile
(population) *(area)* *(population density)*

7. Russia's population is 146,393,569 people, and its area is 6,592,800 square miles.

______________ ÷ ______________ = ____________ people per square mile
(population) *(area)* *(population density)*

8. Japan's population is 126,182,077 people, and its area is 145,882 square miles.

______________ ÷ ______________ = ____________ people per square mile
(population) *(area)* *(population density)*

Name ______________________ Date ______________

The Cold War and the End of the Soviet Union

Directions **Complete this graphic organizer by filling in facts and outcomes about the Cold War.**

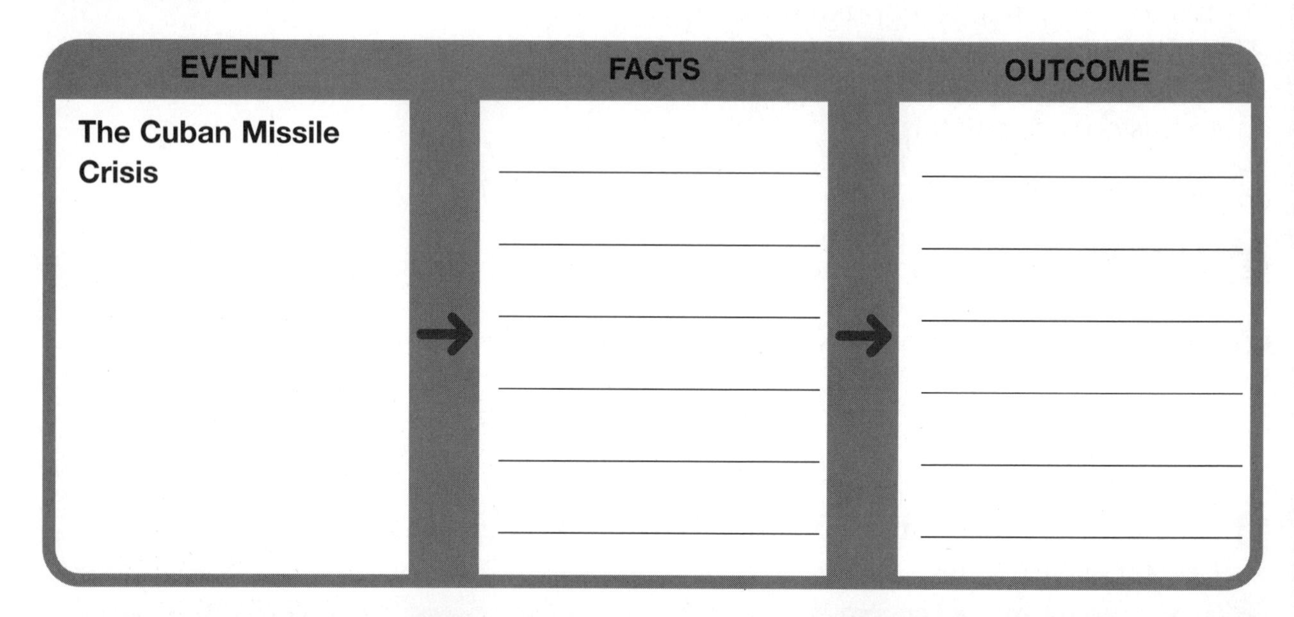

EVENT	FACTS	OUTCOME
The Cuban Missile Crisis		

EVENT	FACTS	OUTCOME
Mikhail Gorbachev becomes the leader of the Soviet Union.		

Use after reading Chapter 16, pages 578–603.

· CHAPTER ·

16

Name ______________________ Date ______________

Test Preparation

Directions **Read each question and choose the best answer. Then fill in the circle for the answer you have chosen. be sure to fill in the circle completely.**

1. In an arms race, nations compete to—
   - Ⓐ sell the most weapons.
   - Ⓑ use the most weapons.
   - Ⓒ build the most weapons.
   - Ⓓ destroy the most weapons.

2. In the case *Brown v. Board of Education of Topeka* the United States Supreme Court decided that—
   - Ⓕ all cities must set up public school systems.
   - Ⓖ segregation on school buses is unconstitutional.
   - Ⓗ segregated schools cannot offer an equal education.
   - Ⓙ all teachers must receive equal pay, no matter what their race is.

3. Sandra Day O'Connor was the first woman to—
   - Ⓐ orbit Earth and walk on the moon.
   - Ⓑ run for President of the United States.
   - Ⓒ serve as a United States Supreme Court justice.
   - Ⓓ fight for the rights of migrant workers.

4. What was the Great Society?
   - Ⓕ an organization that fought for civil rights for African Americans
   - Ⓖ President Johnson's plan to improve the lives of Americans
   - Ⓗ the United States' strategy to force Cuba to get rid of its Soviet missiles
   - Ⓙ an organization that encouraged people to visit the United States

5. How did President George Bush respond when Iraq invaded Kuwait?
   - Ⓐ He pulled all United States troops out of Vietnam.
   - Ⓑ He convinced the leaders of Egypt and Israel to sign a peace treaty.
   - Ⓒ He called Iraq "an evil empire."
   - Ⓓ He organized Operation Desert Storm.

Name ______________________________ Date ____________

The American People Today

Directions **Choose two of the items shown. Write a paragraph explaining the effect that each item has had on life in the United States. Describe what life might be like without the item.**

____

____

____

____

____

____

____

____

____

____

____

(continued)

Use after reading Chapter 17, Lesson 1, pages 620–625.

Name ______________________ Date ______________

Directions **Use the clues to complete the word puzzle. The letters in the outlined box will spell a word that describes a characteristic of the United States population.**

Clues

1. Many people who come to live in the United States are looking for ______ and opportunity.
2. More than 1 million ______ came to the United States during the 1990s.
3. The United States population grows when more people are born and when more people ______ to this country.
4. The Sun ______ stretches across the southern United States.
5. Texas and ______ have the largest Hispanic populations.
6. Currently, most people who come to live in the United States are from Latin American or ______ countries.
7. Of the 20 percent of United States school children who do not speak English at home, most speak ______.
8. A group of people from the same country, of the same race, or with the same culture is called a(n) ______ group.
9. A decade is a period of ten ______.

1 ___ ___ ___ ___ [ ] ___ ___

2 ___ ___ ___ [ ] ___ ___ ___ ___ ___ ___

3 ___ ___ [ ] ___

4 ___ [ ] ___ ___

5 ___ ___ ___ ___ ___ ___ [ ] ___ ___ ___

6 ___ [ ] ___ ___ ___

7 ___ ___ ___ ___ [ ] ___ ___

8 ___ [ ] ___ ___ ___ ___

9 [ ] ___ ___ ___ ___

Name ______________________ Date ____________

CHART AND GRAPH SKILLS

Use a Cartogram

The cartogram below shows the population of North America.

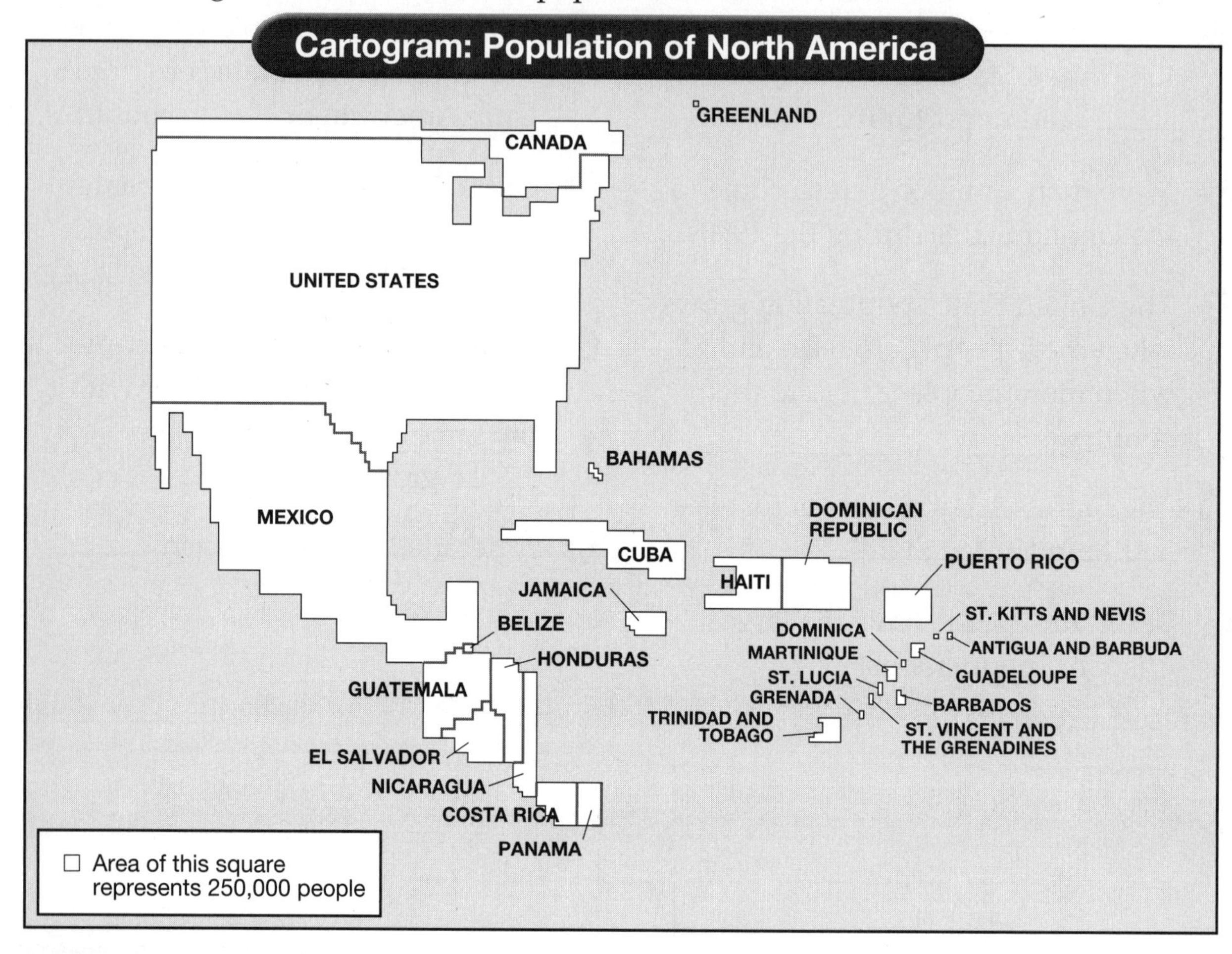

Directions **Write a brief paragraph that defines the term *population cartogram,* and discusses appropriate and inappropriate uses of a population cartogram.**

____

____

____

____

____

____

(continued)

Use after reading Chapter 17, Skill Lesson, pages 626–627.

Name ______________________ Date ______________

Directions **Use the population cartogram of North America on the previous page and a political map of North America from your textbook to answer the following questions. Remember that Puerto Rico is a territory of the United States.**

1. Which country has the largest population? ______________________

2. What country has the second largest population? ______________________

3. Which country has the greatest land area? ______________________

4. Which country has the smaller population, Cuba or Jamaica?

   ____

5. Which is larger: the population of Canada or the population of Mexico?

   ____

6. Which country has the larger population, Cost Rico or Belize?

   ____

7. Which two countries have the largest populations? ______________________

   ____

8. What does the size of Mexico on the cartogram tell you about the population of Mexico? ______________________

9. What does the size of Canada on the cartogram and on the map tell you about the population of Canada? ______________________

   ____

Name ______________________ Date ______________

The Challenges of Growth

Directions **The table shows six challenges that face a growing population. Write each solution from the list below in the appropriate box in the table. Some challenges will have more than one solution. Some solutions may help solve more than one challenge.**

Solutions

add more bus routes

adjust number of seats in Congress to match current states' populations

build rapid-transit systems

pass laws to protect endangered species

improve public transportation

prevent building on some land

recycle glass, metal, plastic, and paper

use electronic highway signs

use computer-controlled traffic lights

pass laws to stop land and water pollution

improve technology

Challenges	Solutions
1 Damage to wildlife	
2 Large amounts of trash	
3 Demands on natural resources	
4 Keeping government fair	
5 Roads jammed with cars and trucks	

Use after reading Chapter 17, Lesson 2, pages 628–631.

Name ______________________________ Date ______________

The American Economy

Directions **Use the terms from the lesson to solve the crossword puzzle.**

Across

1. A period when people can find and share rapidly-growing knowledge
3. Buying products on the Internet
4. An economy that is not based on just one kind of industry
7. Buying and selling between companies in more than one country
8. Businesses that rely on each other for resources, products, or services

Down

2. A promise between nations not to tax the products that they buy from or sell to each other
5. An economy that includes businesses from around the world
6. Businesses that design, produce, or use electronic equipment

Use after reading Chapter 17, Lesson 3, pages 632–637.

Name ______________________ Date ____________

Government and the People

Directions **Complete the Web page below by filling in certain responsibilities of United States citizens. The home page on the left lists some constitutional rights. Use the items below to fill in the pop-up windows with citizens' matching responsibilities.**

- Stay informed about local, state, and national events; respect the views of others
- Register and take part in local, state, and national elections
- Treat others fairly
- Be willing to serve on a jury

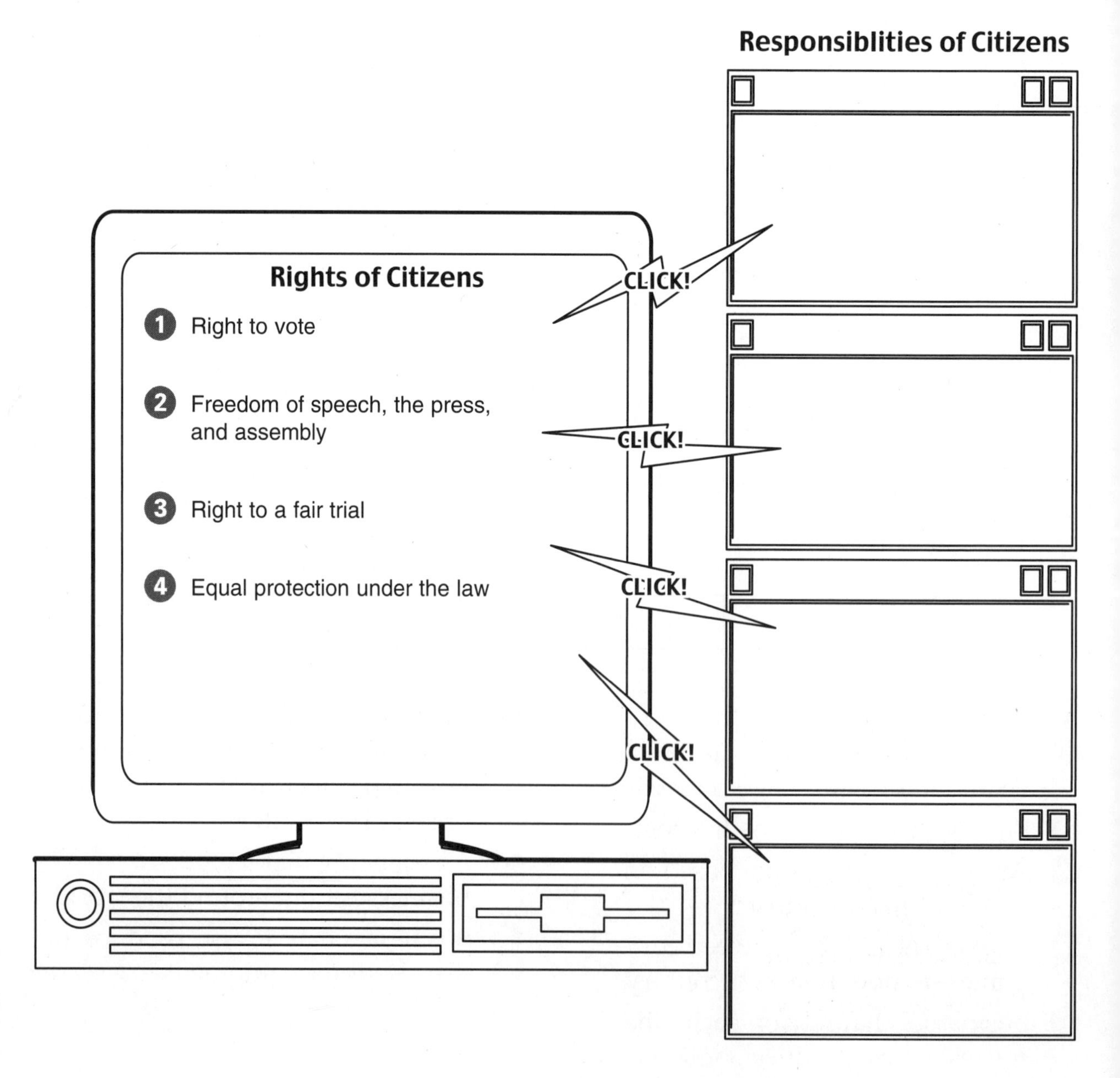

Use after reading Chapter 17, Lesson 4, pages 638–643.

Name ______________________________ Date ______________

CITIZENSHIP SKILLS

Identify Political Symbols

Directions **Match each symbol below with the appropriate description. Write the letter of the description on the line next to the symbol. Some descriptions will be used more than once.**

a. United States government

b. Democratic party

c. United States Congress

d. Republican party

e. President of the United States

f. The United States of America

g. freedom

1.  ______

2.  ______

3.   ______

4.  ______

5.  ______

6.  ______

7.  ______

8.  ______

Name ______________________ Date ____________

Facts and Opinions About the United States

Directions **Complete this graphic organizer by identifying facts and opinions about the United States.**

THE POPULATION OF THE UNITED STATES

FACT		OPINION
More than 291 million people live in the United States.	→	______
______	→	______

THE UNITED STATES GOVERNMENT AND THE PEOPLE

FACT		OPINION
______	→	______
______	→	______

Use after reading Chapter 17, pages 619–647.

·CHAPTER·

17

Name ______________________ Date ____________

Test Preparation

Directions **Read each question and choose the best answer. Then fill in the circle for the answer you have chosen. Be sure to fill in the circle completely.**

1. Today, from where do most immigrants to the United States come?
   - Ⓐ Asia and Europe
   - Ⓑ Africa and Europe
   - Ⓒ Asia and Latin America
   - Ⓓ Africa and Latin America

2. How can a rapid-transit system prevent traffic jams?
   - Ⓕ by providing people with alternate ways to travel
   - Ⓖ by adding traffic lights to highways
   - Ⓗ by adding more highways
   - Ⓙ by limiting the number of people who travel by train

3. Which is an example of a service job?
   - Ⓐ miner
   - Ⓑ nurse
   - Ⓒ farmer
   - Ⓓ carpenter

4. In a free-enterprise economy, which is a result of an increased demand for a product?
   - Ⓕ The price of the product will go up.
   - Ⓖ The supply of the product will grow.
   - Ⓗ Fewer people will want to buy the product.
   - Ⓙ Fewer companies will want to sell the product.

5. What is the role of the federal government?
   - Ⓐ To organize the two main political parties
   - Ⓑ To oversee the work of the state governments
   - Ⓒ To stop local laws from conflicting with state laws
   - Ⓓ To make and apply the laws that run the United States

Name ______________________________ Date ______________

Mexico

Directions **Write the letter next to each event listed below in the appropriate place on the time line.**

a. In the early 1900s, Mexican leaders write a new constitution that includes land for farmers and a six-year limit on presidents' terms.

b. Soon after the Mexico economy starts to recover, Mexico elects its first president from the Partido Acción Nacional (PAN), Vicente Fox.

c. United States President George W. Bush meets with Mexican President Vicente Fox to show the importance of ties between the two nations.

d. In the late 1900s Mexico, Canada, and the United States sign the North American Free Trade Agreement (NAFTA).

e. In the 1820s part of Spain's army helps Mexico win its independence.

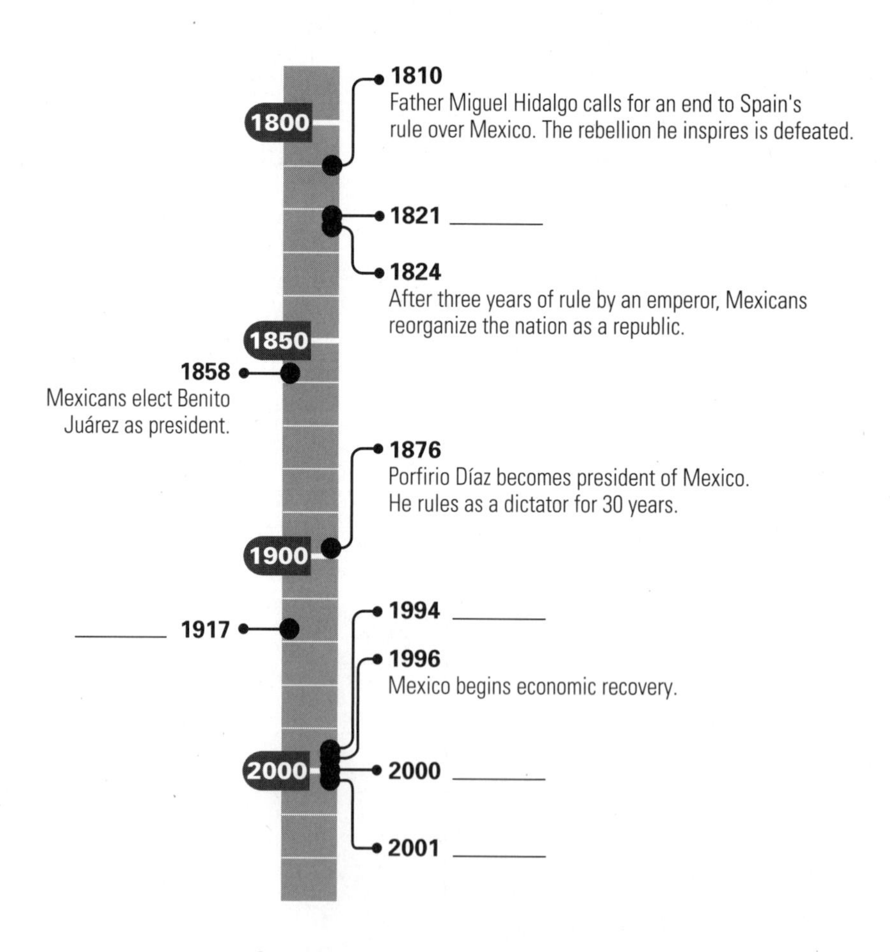

Use after reading Chapter 18, Lesson 1, pages 652–656.

Name ______________________ Date ______________

Central America and the Caribbean

Directions **Answer the questions below.**

1. What seven countries make up Central America? ______________________

____

2. What crops are grown in the countries of Central America?

____

3. Which natural events challenge the residents of islands in the Caribbean?

____

____

4. What kind of government does Cuba have? ______________________

5. Which Caribbean islands are part of the United States? ______________________

____

6. How is the government of Costa Rica similar to the government of the United States? ______________________

____

Name ______________________ Date ____________

CHART AND GRAPH SKILLS

How to Read Population Pyramids

Directions Study the population pyramid of Costa Rica below. Then write a paragraph that explains to another student what the pyramid reveals about the population of Costa Rica. As you write, try to answer these questions:

1. What is a population pyramid?
2. Which part of the pyramid is the largest? What does this mean?
3. Which part of the pyramid is the smallest? What does this mean?
4. Does the pyramid show any differences between females and males?
5. About how many Costa Ricans are in your age group?

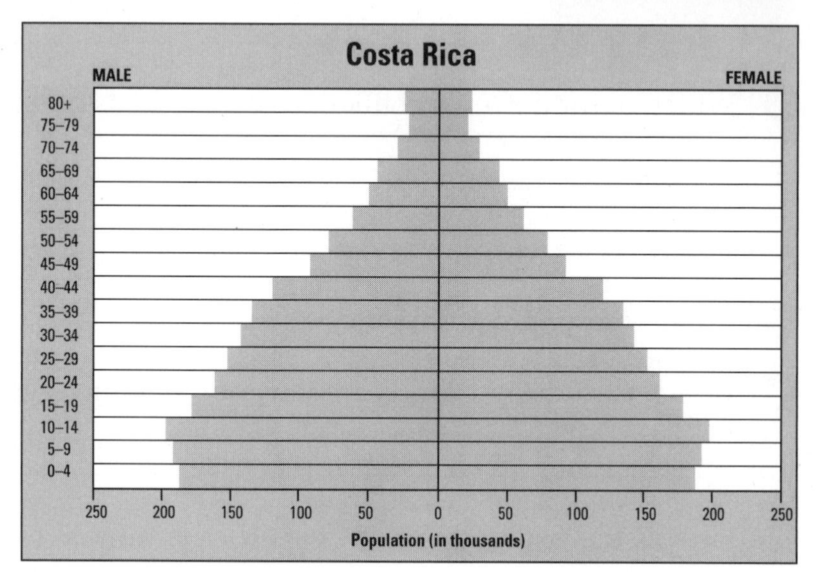

___

___

___

___

___

___

___

___

___

___

(continued)

Use after reading Chapter 18, Skill Lesson, pages 662–663.

Name ______________________________ Date ______________

Directions **The population pyramid on the left represents the population of Mexico in 1980. The population pyramid on the right illustrates what the Mexican population might look like in 2030. Use the information from the two pyramids to answer the questions below.**

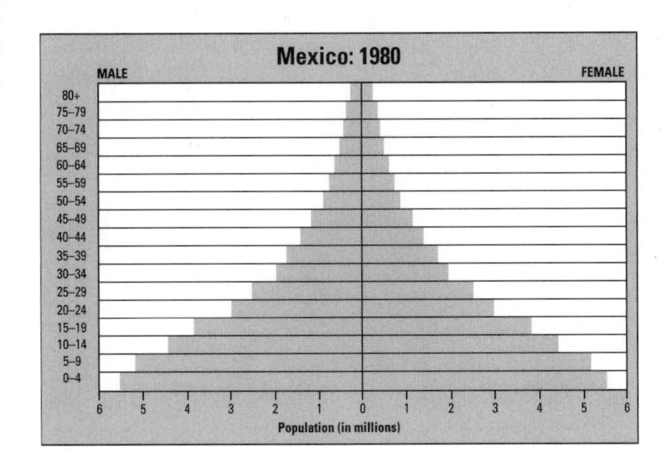

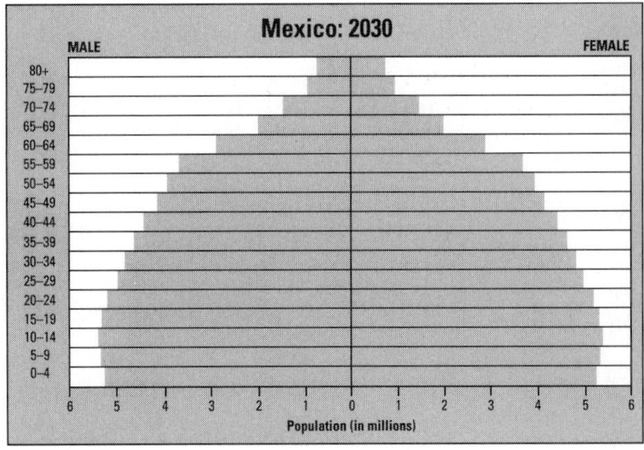

6. About how many people were 20–24 years old in 1980? ______________

   in 2030? ______________

7. Which gender/age group was the smallest in 1980? ______________

   in 2030? ______________

8. Which gender/age-group is the largest in 1980? ______________

   in 2030? ______________

9. What is the predicted approximate increase in the number of people 50–54 years old between 1980 and 2030? ______________

10. Do any gender/age groups show a predicted decrease between 1980 and 2030?

    ____

    If so, which one(s)? ______________

11. About how many people were less than 15 years old in 1980?

    ____

Name ______________________________ Date ______________

South America

Directions Read each statement below. If the statement is true, write *T* in the blank. If the statement is false, write *F* in the blank.

1. ______ Most of South America is covered in tropical rain forest.
2. ______ Scientists feel that it is important to preserve the rain forests of South America because of their potential medical benefits.
3. ______ At one time Spain controlled all of South America.
4. ______ All *mestizos* come from South America.
5. ______ The American and French revolutions encouraged people in South American colonies to fight for their independence.
6. ______ Simón Bolívar was one of the leaders of the efforts to free South American colonies.
7. ______ Simón Bolívar believed that the former South American colonies had so much in common that they could join together as a single nation.
8. ______ In the new, independent countries of South America, dictators or armies often took control of the political process.
9. ______ Reformers in South America have worked to help small farmers own their land.

Use after reading Chapter 18, Lesson 3, pages 664–668.

Name ______________________ Date ____________

Canada

Directions **Circle the letter of the best answer.**

1. Which best represents the flag of Canada?

A. 
B. 
C. 
D. 

2. Which is a prairie province of Canada?

F. Alberta
G. Quebec
H. Ontario
J. Nunavut

3. Which ocean does **not** border Canada?

A. Arctic
B. Indian
C. Pacific
D. Atlantic

4. Which best describes the relationship between Canada and Great Britain right after the North America Act of 1867?

F. Independent nation
G. Conquered territory
H. Commonwealth partner
J. Representative government

5. Who is the official leader of the executive branch of the Canadian government?

A. The Parliament
B. The Prime Minister
C. The British monarch
D. The governor-general

6. Who runs the executive branch of the Canadian government on a day-to-day basis?

F. The Parliament
G. The Prime Minister
H. The British monarch
J. The governor-general

7. Which nation buys the majority of Canada's exports?

A. France
B. Australia
C. Great Britain
D. the United States

Use after reading Chapter 18, Lesson 4, pages 669–673.

Name ____________________ Date ____________

MAP AND GLOBE SKILLS

Use a Time Zone Map

Directions **Use the time zone map below to answer the questions.**

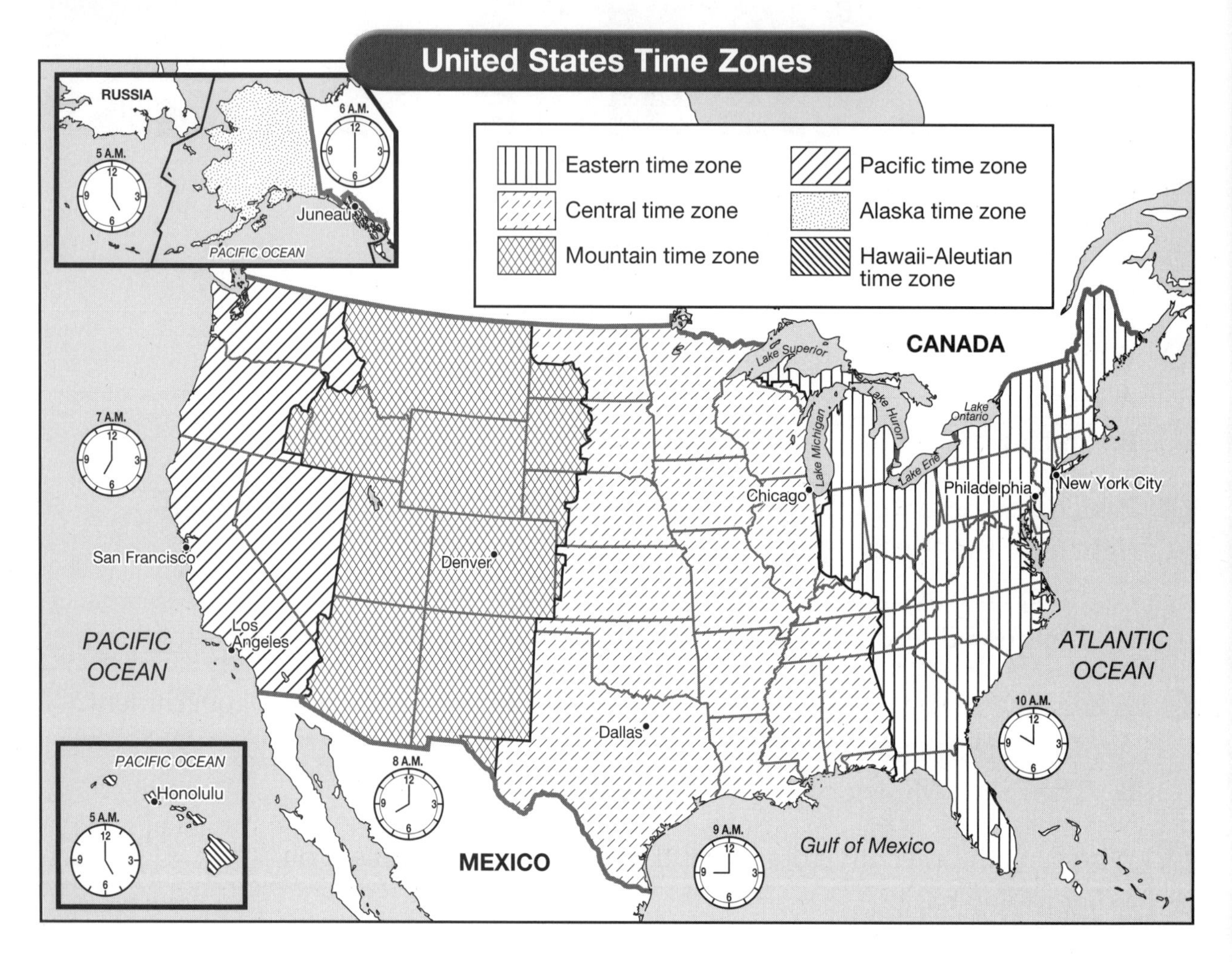

1. How many time zones cover the 50 states? ____________________

2. Which of these cities are in the Central time zone: Chicago, Dallas, Denver?

____

3. When it is 8:00 A.M. in New York City, what time is it in Los Angeles?

____

4. When it is 3:30 P.M. in Chicago, what time is it in Honolulu?

____

(continued)

Use after reading Chapter 18, Skill Lesson, pages 674–675.

Name ______________________________ Date ______________

Directions **Use the time zone map to complete the chart below.**

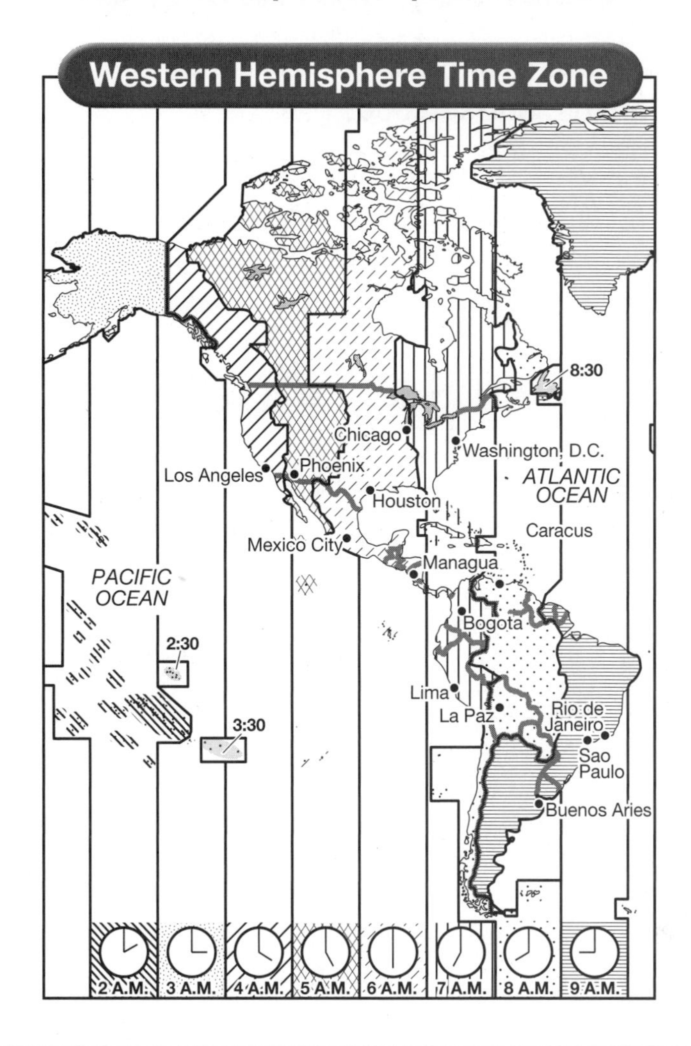

When the time is . . .	The time is . . .
5 2:00 A.M. in Buenos Aires	______________ in Chicago
6 1:00 P.M. in São Paulo	______________ in La Paz
7 6:30 A.M. in Los Angeles	______________ in Lima
8 3:45 P.M. in Houston	______________ in Bogotá
9 2:00 P.M. in Rio de Janeiro	______________ in Phoenix
10 11:30 A.M. in Managua	______________ in Mexico City
11 9:15 P.M. in Caracas	______________ in Washington, D.C.

Name ______________________________ Date ______________

The United States, Canada, and Mexico

Directions **Complete this graphic organizer by comparing and contrasting the United States, Canada, and Mexico.**

THE UNITED STATES AND CANADA		THE UNITED STATES AND MEXICO	

SIMILARITIES	**DIFFERENCES**	**SIMILARITIES**	**DIFFERENCES**
Both Canada and the United States were once under British rule.	______	**Mexico and the United States both have democratic governments.**	______

Use after reading Chapter 18, pages 651–677.

• CHAPTER •

18

Name ______________________________ Date ______________

Test Preparation

Directions **Read each question and choose the best answer. Then fill in the circle for the answer you have chosen. Be sure to fill in the circle completely.**

1. Which two civilizations have created the cultural heritage of Mexico?
   - Ⓐ PRI and PAN
   - Ⓑ *Mestizo* and French
   - Ⓒ Native American and Spanish
   - Ⓓ North American and South American

2. Which do many of the Central American and Caribbean nations have in common?
   - Ⓕ Land area
   - Ⓖ Population size
   - Ⓗ Threat of hurricanes
   - Ⓙ Communist governments

3. Which word best describes the political history of Haiti?
   - Ⓐ Isolated
   - Ⓑ Unstable
   - Ⓒ Communist
   - Ⓓ Democratic

4. Which person led the efforts to free parts of South America from colonial rule?
   - Ⓕ Fidel Castro
   - Ⓖ Simón Bolívar
   - Ⓗ Jean-Bertrand Aristide
   - Ⓙ Father Miguel Hidalgo

5. Which two nations in the Western Hemisphere share a border of more than 5,000 miles?
   - Ⓐ Colombia and Brazil
   - Ⓑ Colombia and Panama
   - Ⓒ United States and Mexico
   - Ⓓ United States and Canada